Appalachian Fiddle

By Miles Krassen

© 1973
Oak Publications, New York
Music Sales Limited, London

PHOTOGRAPHS:
Ray Alden: Page 32
Ray Alden/Dave Spilkia: Pages 66 and 88
John Cohen: Page 14
Carl Fleischhauer: Page 55
David Gahr: Pages 40, and 49
Alan Jabbour: Page 71
Rip Springfield: Pages 6, 7, 8, and 9
Arthur Tress: Pages 52 and 78

COVER PHOTOGRAPH: Jimmy Natural Meyers of
Five Forks, Va., taken by Doug Crosswhite

Book design by Mei Mei Sanford

©1973 Oak Publications
A Division of Embassy Music Corporation
33 West 60th Street, New York 10023

Music Sales Limited, 78 Newman Street, W.I. E 4JZ, London

International Standard Book Number 0-8256-0141-X
Library of Congress Card Catalogue Number 72-96103

Contents

Preface, 4
Introduction, 5

The Four Keys, 10
    Soldier's Joy, 15
    Shortenin' Bread, 15
    Ida Red, 16
    Old Joe Clark, 16
Double Stops, 17
Double Note Fingering Chart, 18
    Barlow Knife, 25
    Barlow Knife (double noting), 26
    Angeline, 26
    Angeline (double noting), 27
    Dinah, 28
    Dinah (double noting), 29
    West Fork Girls, 30
    Boogerman, 30
    Old Molly Hare, 31
Modal Tunes, 32
    Ducks on the Pond, 33
    Kitchen Girl, 34
    June Apple, 34
    Cluck Old Hen, 35
    28th of January, 36
    Salt River, 37
    Lonesome John, 38
    Cold Frosty Morning, 38
    West Virginia Girls, 39
    Yew Piney Mountain, 41
Breakdowns in D, 42
    Forked Deer, 43
    Arkansas Traveler, 44
    Soldier's Joy, 45
    Fortune, 46
    Backstep Cindy, 47
    Ragtime Annie, 48

    Eighth of January, 50
    Blackeyed Susan, 51
    Dusty Miller, 53
    Quince Dillon's High D Tune, 54
G Tunes, 55
    Red Fox, 56
    Jawbone, 57
    Cumberland Gap, 58
    Silly Bill, 59
    Blackberry Blossom, 60
    Stoney Point, 61
    Teetotaler, 62
    Ebenezer, 63
    Sandy River Belle, 64
    Roundtown Girls, 65
Tunes in A and C, 66
    Brown's Dream, 66
    Bill Cheatem, 68
    Boatsman, 69
    Money Musk, 70
    Fire on the Mountain, 72
    Grey Eagle, 73
    Billy in the Low Ground, 74
    East Tennessee Blues, 75
    Wagoner, 76
    Row's Division, 77
Hornpipes, 78
    Fisher's Hornpipe, 79
    Rickett's Hornpipe, 80
    Red Haired Boy, 81
    Durang's Hornpipe, 82
    Sailor's Hornpipe, 83
    George Booker, 84
    Mountain Hornpipe, 85
    Haste to the Wedding, 86

Discography, 87

Preface

My interest in mountain music began in the early 1960's when I first heard the New Lost City Ramblers in Philadelphia. At first I concentrated on learning to play the banjo. But the fiddle appealed to me more and by 1963 I was learning to play it. I had no teacher. I began by learning to play the tunes that the Ramblers had recorded. As my interest grew, I met collectors of old records made by mountain bands in the 1920's. These recordings broadened my knowledge of country music but gave me the false impression that Old Time Music had ceased being played seriously during the 1930's.

Fortunately, I heard about fiddlers' conventions that were held in the Southern Appalachians. In the Spring of 1964, I went to the Old Fiddlers' Convention at Union Grove, N.C. Here, for the first time, I heard mountain music played by living traditional fiddlers. The experience was a revelation to me. Music was still being played which was very much like that recorded on the old records and sometimes played even better. Since my first trip to the mountains, I have concentrated on the music of living Appalachian fiddlers.

My first teacher and greatest influence as a fiddler was Franklin George of Bluefield, West Virginia. Frank knows many fine rare tunes which he plays in a beautiful lilting style. For several years I practiced playing those tunes I could learn from Frank and other Appalachian fiddlers. Gradually, as I became more comfortable playing this style, I began to develop my own versions of tunes.

The music of traditional Appalachian fiddlers goes beyond the world of commercial country music of any period. The more I listened to the music of fiddlers like Frank George and Charlie Higgins the more I realized that many of the best tunes have never been recorded commercially. The music of some of the most exceptional fiddlers has never been heard outside a small area in the mountains.

It is my hope that this book will help spread greater awareness of the music of the Southern Appalachian fiddlers. Especially, I hope the book will be of use to those who would like to be a part of this great living tradition.

Introduction

Learning to fiddle

Most of the fiddlers I have met in the Southern Appalachians did not read music. Certainly, none of them learned to play from a book. In fact, it is quite common to hear a fiddler express the opinion that fiddle tunes can't be written in notes. This is a sentiment which I largely share. It is no more possible to learn to be a good fiddler simply by reading notes than it is to become a good writer by reading a dictionary. You must hear a good deal of music and develop a feeling for it before you can begin to play. So, if you haven't yet been exposed to fiddling, I suggest that you turn to the discography at the end of this book and listen to as many of the recordings as possible before proceeding.

Fiddle music has almost always been transmitted by living example. Due to the nature of their dissemination, the tunes, themselves, remain organic and alive. Many fiddlers will claim, mischievously, to know the correct or oldest version of a tune. But in reality the unwritten nature of the tunes and the aural learning process allow considerable freedom for subjective factors to affect performances. The best fiddlers I have heard always adopted several ways of varying their favorite tunes. It is characteristic of Appalachian fiddling that the tunes always remain identifiable, but the actual choice of notes, bowing patterns, and phrasing can vary from performance to performance.

In the chapters ahead we will be looking at transcriptions of fiddle tunes in more or less common versions. There are also selected examples of various ways that fine fiddlers cast their mark on a tune. Among fiddlers mere uniqueness is not necessarily a virtue. These examples illustrate the use of an individual's creativity within traditional forms.

Written examples of fiddle tunes have existed in the British Isles at least since the seventeenth century. I have known several excellent old time fiddlers who were familiar with Cole's "1001 Fiddle Tunes" or O'Neill's "Music of Ireland." Collections of this sort have all the usefulness of a dictionary or encyclopedia. Sometime, you may find yourself trying to recall a tune that a fiddler played who is 1000 miles away. If you can read music, the notes in the book might help you.

Frank George used to tell me, when I asked him to teach me a tune, that the best way to learn was to listen first and then go off and whistle the tune to yourself for several days before trying to play it. This is really an ideal method of learning. And it can be profitable, whether the source of the tune is a fiddler you know, a record, or even the notes in a book. If you whistle a tune until you can really enjoy it, you won't go wrong when you set about to play it. The point is, in approaching the transcriptions of fiddle tunes, always use the notes just enough to get the tune into your head. *Then,* learn to play it. A fiddle tune is always something more than any particular set of notes!

This book is designed to make the subtleties of fiddling more accessible to people who are not necessarily in an area where fiddlers are plentiful. As you get further into the music you will surely want to meet some accomplished fiddlers. Fiddlers' Conventions are always a good place to find them. (Each spring The Library of Congress, Archives of American Folk Song, publishes a list of conventions held during the summer.) While nothing can ever replace the direct learning experience, a wise use of and familiarity with the materials in this book should well prepare you for the encounter.

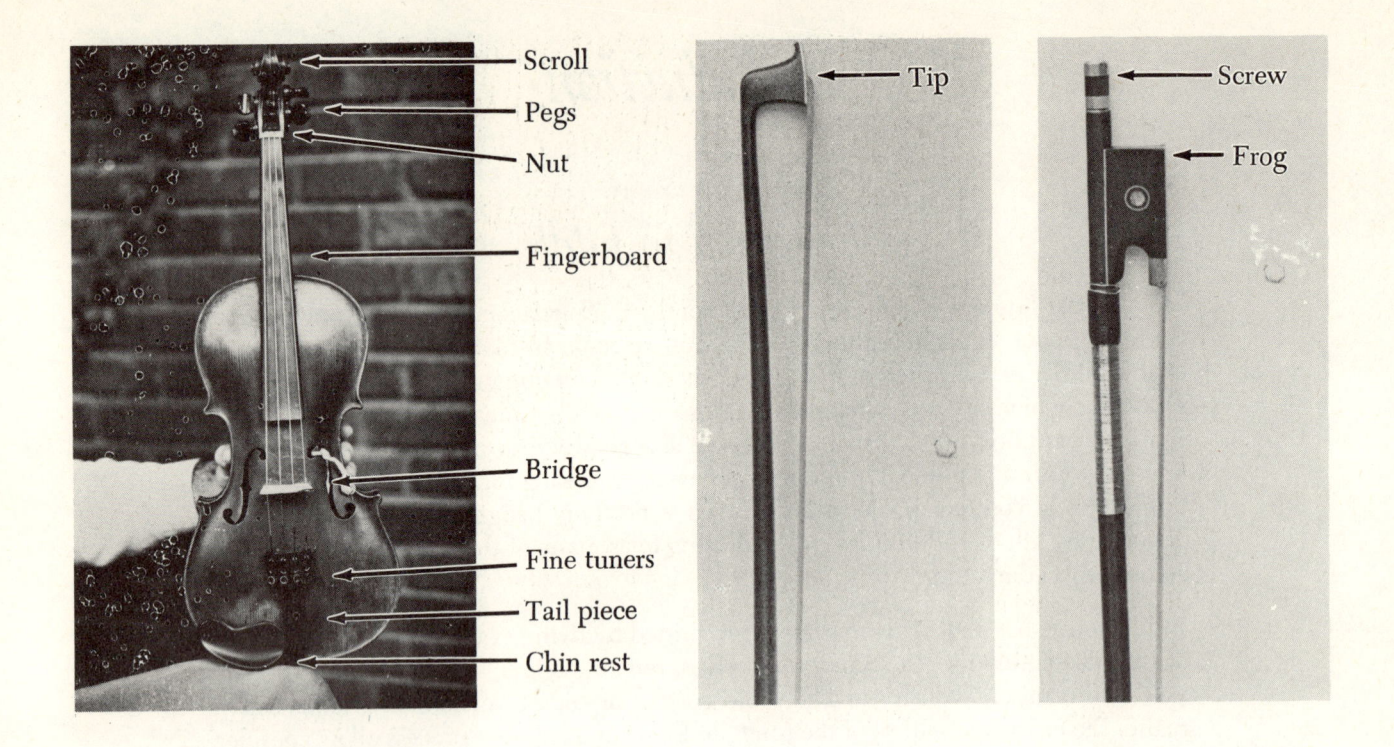

What is a fiddle?

The instruments played in the Appalachians range from the crude homemade to the original of an old European master violin maker. The late French Carpenter of Clay County, West Virginia, claimed that his fiddle was an original Jacob Steiner and people were always coming down from the city trying to persuade him to part with it. Basically, good fiddlers appreciate the quality of a well made violin. But when you are just learning, even a Stradivarius won't sound like much. Almost any violin will do for a start. The important thing is how it is adjusted. When you get to the point where you are sure that the unpleasant sound of your fiddling is not your own fault, you are ready for a better instrument.

The prices of violins are not necessarily commensurate with their quality. Prices vary greatly in different parts of the country and depend on local economic factors and demand. There are still a lot of good old fiddles around that are not being played and can be acquired inexpensively. The best places to find them are at country auctions and antique stores or from fiddlers' widows. You might be taking a risk, but every so often one can walk away with a real bargain. If you approach a violin maker you should be prepared to pay a higher price, but you will be more confident regarding the quality of the instrument.

There are only two real differences between a fiddle and a violin: how the instrument is adjusted and the way it is played. If you get your instrument from a violinist or violin maker, the first thing you do to transform it into a fiddle is to *reshape the bridge*. A violinist uses a bridge with a high arch so that his bow will not accidentally catch more than one string at a time. Most fiddle styles make great use of playing two strings at once. Consequently, fiddlers *flatten* their bridges so that just enough arch is left for single string playing when required. It should be stressed that the shaping of the bridge remains a most important element when adjusting it to a fiddle.

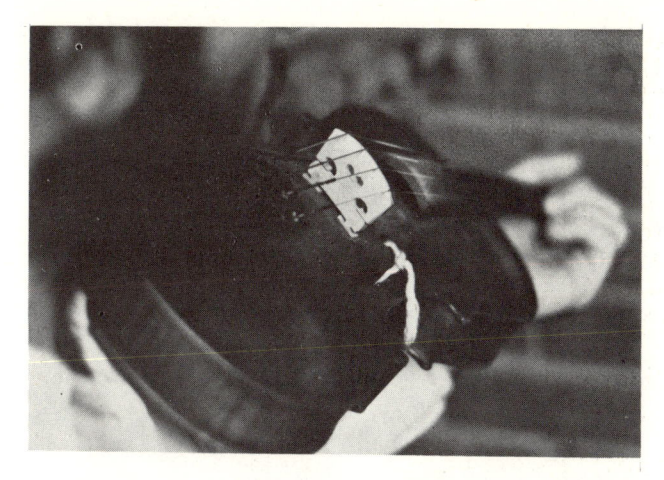

When I first began meeting fiddlers I was amazed how effortlessly they could play so many notes at fast tempos. Much of this facility is the reward of practice, but the adjustment of the fiddle also has an effect. When I showed Frank George my first fiddle he laughed.

"No one could fiddle on that thing!"

The bridge was much too arched and the strings were more than half an inch above the fingerboard. The strings were so high that it took more will power than strength of hand to finger the notes. It is wise when cutting the bridge to have the strings as close to the fingerboard as possible.

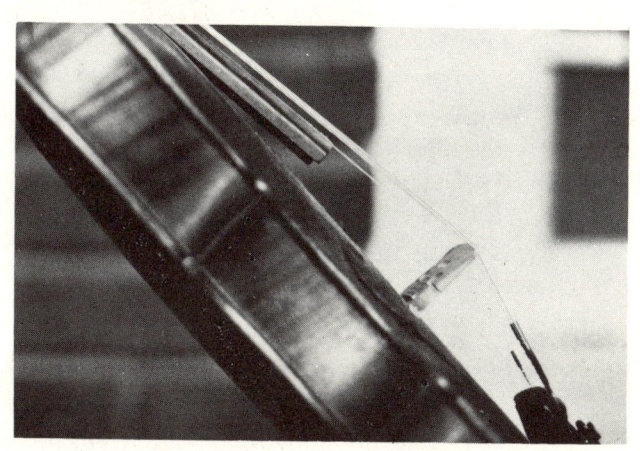

French Carpenter had his strings so low you could hardly see them from the side. But be careful. If the strings are too close to the fingerboard, you will be unable to sound the correct intonation of the notes near the nut; for example, F♯ and G on your E string. This problem sometimes is also caused by a worn out nut needing replacement.

Watch out for old fiddles that no longer have their necks set correctly. If the angle of the fingerboard has leveled off, you would have to cut the bridge too short and stubby in order to adjust the strings. These fiddles require a resetting of the necks, or the angle of the fingerboard raised. A too-short bridge will impair the tone quality.

Most fiddlers use steel strings. They sound louder than the gut strings that violinists favor. Volume is very important when playing with a banjo and guitar. Since vibrato is rarely used in fiddling dance tunes, the quick response of steel strings is desirable; they seem easier to play in tune. A very good set is made by Super-Sensitive. Many of the older fiddlers prefer the cheaper Black Diamond strings. Whichever you choose, you will want to place fine tuners in your tailpiece for each of the strings. Purists may object, but it can be bothersome trying to tune steel strings precisely with violin friction pegs.

If you have some extra money to spend, get a good bow. It is remarkable how much a bow has to do with tone quality. A good hand-made bow will improve the sound of almost any fiddle. For bows, it is wise to consult a violin maker. You may have to spend twice as much for your bow as for your fiddle but it is worth it.

If you really want to play the fiddle, don't be discouraged if your instrument is not the finest. I've heard pretty good music played on cigar box fiddles. Just make sure your fiddle is well-adjusted and don't believe what you read on the labels.

How to hold a fiddle

I have always found it best to hold my fiddle under my chin, propped against the collarbone. The position is basically the same as a violinist's except the left arm is kept lower. Some fiddlers do rest their fiddles further down on their chest. However, this position restricts fingering ability because the left hand has to contribute more to balancing the fiddle. When you hold a fiddle under the chin it will stay there even if you take your left hand away.

The chest position is perfectly adequate and a comfortable one for playing simple dance tunes that do not require playing higher than the first position. Sometimes, if I am playing for a square dance when a simple tune has to be played very fast and repeated for ten or fifteen minutes, I'll let my fiddle drop down on my chest and watch the dancers. When you play a tune for five or six minutes straight, it becomes effortless. But when I play a hornpipe or one of the more complicated tunes which require intricate fingering and even playing up the neck, it means business and I have to tuck my fiddle under the chin. If you learn to play with the fiddle under your chin, you can be sure, no matter what your goals are as a fiddler, your technique will not be hampered by the way you hold a fiddle.

For the same reason, it is best to learn to *arch* the fingers of your left hand over the fingerboard. This way you can depress the strings with your fingertips. Many fiddlers do quite well holding their fiddle in the palm of the hand and noting with flattened fingers. But I have found that fiddlers who play this way are often excellent at hoedowns but can rarely meet the demands of a hornpipe. These more difficult tunes require precise fingering of many notes. They are played by the best fiddlers in a style that employs the old Celtic ornaments like triplets and trills. Almost every fiddler I have met who uses this technique arched his fingers.

There are probably more ways of holding the bow adequately than of holding the fiddle. Some fiddlers grip the stick above the frog. Others grasp the bow at the end, more like a violinist. Frank George keeps his little finger behind the screw, curls his first three fingers over the wood, and places his thumb between the wood and bow hair, bent into a gap between his first and second fingers. I prefer to keep my thumb flat against the bottom of the frog.

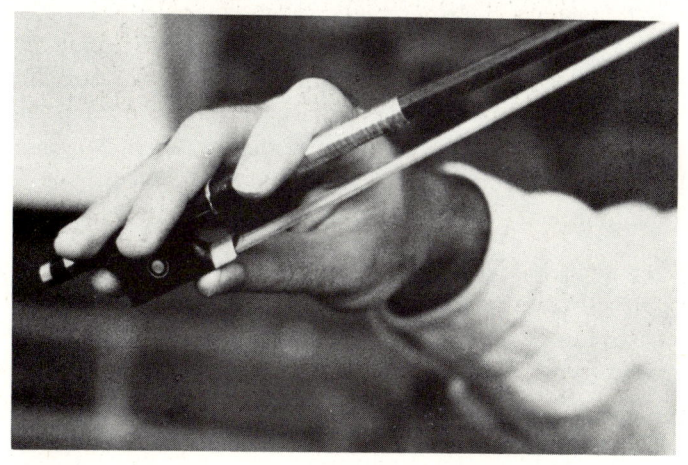

In holding the bow, some modification of the violinist's grip is probably best as it allows freedom for the wrist to snap quick, short bow strokes. The bowing of fiddle tunes can be rather complex and requires a good deal of control to execute smoothly. For the most part, only the upper third of the bow touches the strings. You will find that your bow is better balanced when you grip it at the frog. There are also times when a longer bow stroke is necessary and then it is advantageous to have use of the full length of the bow.

In holding the fiddle and the bow it is very important to find a comfortable position. But it is wise to grow accustomed to one allowing the greatest comfort and freedom as your playing becomes more ambitious.

THE FOUR KEYS

Once you have your fiddle and bow adjusted and held properly, you are ready to begin playing. In the mountains young fiddlers learn to play tunes from the time they are big enough to hold a fiddle. No one that I have met claims to have learned by playing exercises. The attitude of a fiddler always centers on personal satisfaction rather than critical acclaim. Consequently, you can start right in practicing on simple tunes. Technique will come with time and application.

The standard fiddle tuning is G D A E, from the lowest to the highest string:

This is the same tuning violinists use. Later we will discuss other ways of tuning a fiddle. Most fiddle tunes are played in this standard tuning. Some fiddlers use it exclusively. So let's begin with it.

Throughout Europe and the United States the pitch designated A has been standardized at 440 vibrations per second. This is the pitch that pianos and harmonicas are tuned to. Most music stores sell inexpensive pitch pipes which sound this pitch for tuning purposes. In the Appalachians pitch is not standardized. Fiddlers generally tune by ear to a pitch which sounds right to them. It is a common practice for Appalachian fiddlers to tune their strings higher than standard pitch. Sometimes the E string is tuned so high as to sound F or even F♯. High tuning tends to give the fiddle a shriller, tenser tone quality. Fiddlers like Tommy Jarrell and Fred Cockerham always tune high, as do some of the more Irish style fiddlers. I prefer to tune a bit low so that the richer more mellow qualities of the fiddle are emphasized. Of course, when you play with an instrument which cannot alter its pitch like a mouth harp, you will have to tune to it.

No matter what pitch is taken for the A string, standard tuning requires that an interval of a *perfect fifth* exist between any two adjacent strings. This interval is a very common sound in fiddle music when the bow plays two notes at once. In time you will be able to recognize a perfect fifth by ear. But for now, if you can't, it might be best to tune by taking your A string as *Do*, singing up a major scale. When you get to Sol, or the fifth note in the scale, you have sounded the pitch of your E string. Then sing down the scale from A until you get to *Fa*. This is the pitch of your D string. Try tuning the G string by ear.

Most fiddle tunes are played in one of only four keys: G, D, A, and C. Before turning to the tunes themselves, let's run through the notes of the scale for each of these keys or *gears* as they are known in the Appalachians. Once you have learned the fingering for these keys, you will have at your disposal all the notes needed to play just about any fiddle tune. Become as familiar as you can with the finger positions. They must become second nature before you can play by ear.

Here is the notation of a G major scale. The numbers beneath the notes indicate the fingers to be used; 3, for example, means that the pitch is noted by the third finger.

The first and second fingers should also be held down in position on the string. This practice will help you develop a strong left hand and clear intonation. Try to keep your fingers arched as you play.

Key of G:

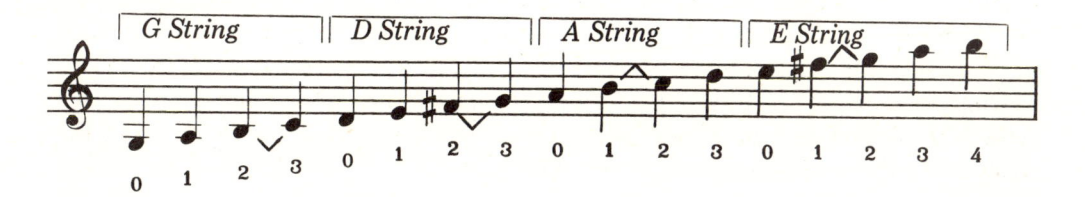

```
        | G String  || D String  || A String  || E String          |
                                                    ♯            ♯
  0   1   2   3   0   1   2   3   0   1   2   3   0   1   2   3   4
```

Note that with the G and D strings your second finger must be close to the third finger. However, when playing the A and E strings, the second finger should be close to the first finger.

The following diagram illustrates the placement of the fingers on the strings for the key of G.

G Major:

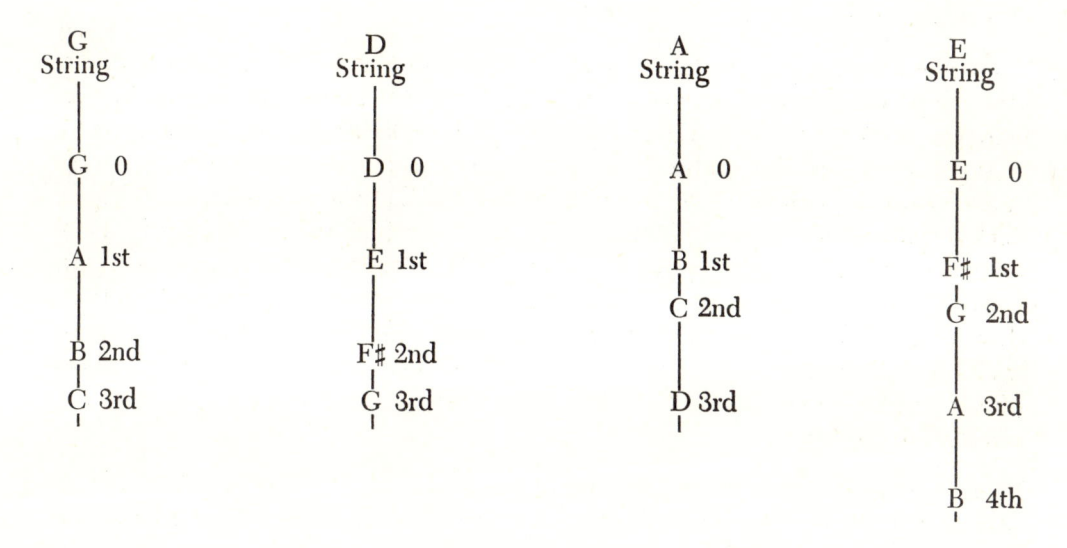

```
G                D                A                E
String           String           String           String
|                |                |                |
G  0             D  0             A  0             E  0
|                |                |                |
A  1st           E  1st           B  1st           F♯ 1st
|                |                |                |
                                  C  2nd           G  2nd
B  2nd           F♯ 2nd                            |
|                |                |                |
C  3rd           G  3rd           D  3rd           A  3rd
|                |                |                |
                                                   B  4th
                                                   |
```

I have only indicated the placement of the fourth finger on the E string. Actually, the fourth finger can be used on any of the strings. If placed properly it will sound the same pitch as the open string to its right. Many fiddlers do not use their fourth finger at all. When necessary, they prefer to slide their third finger up into the fourth finger's position. This is especially effective on the three lower strings. Almost all fiddlers use this sliding third finger technique at some time or other to produce unisons—two strings played simultaneously and sounding the same pitch. Try sliding your third finger up on the A string. Now sound the fingered note with your open E string. You will hear the effect.

Virtually the same sound can be produced with the fourth finger. Since the little finger is usually weaker and more poorly coordinated than the other three, it may take you quite a while before you can use it consistently. However, if you develop an agile fourth finger, you will find it quite a boon for noting some of the more difficult tunes.

Key of D:

In this key the second finger is placed close to the third on the D and A strings and close to the first finger on the E string. Note the fingering on the G string. Here the second finger is in the same position as on the D and A strings. But the third finger must be placed higher for C♯.

D Major:

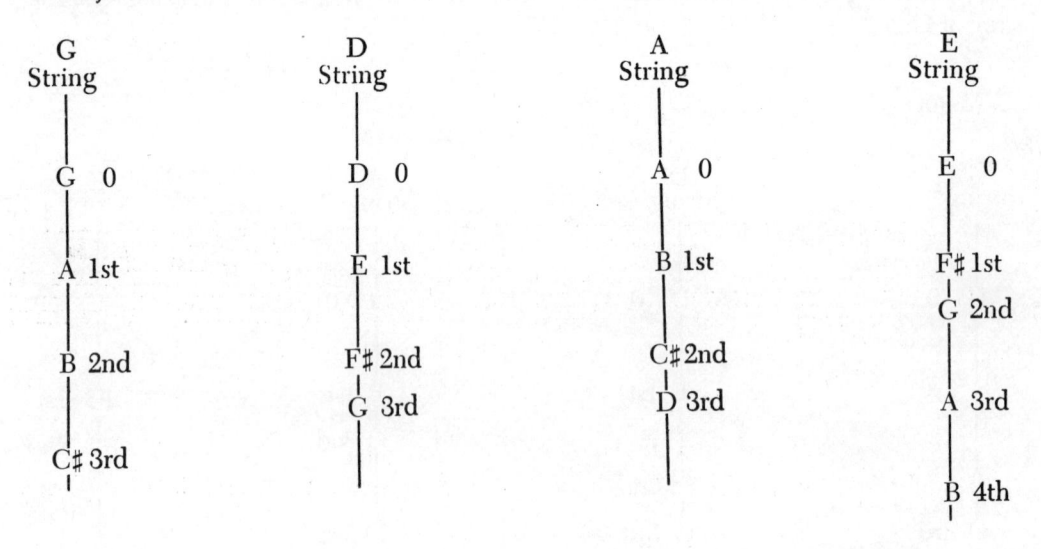

G String	D String	A String	E String
G 0	D 0	A 0	E 0
A 1st	E 1st	B 1st	F♯ 1st
			G 2nd
B 2nd	F♯ 2nd	C♯ 2nd	A 3rd
	G 3rd	D 3rd	
C♯ 3rd			B 4th

Key of A:

In this key the open G string is *not* played. Notice that the first finger has two positions on the G string: the A position as in the keys of G and D and also a G♯ position close to the nut. Give special attention to the position of the second and third finger in this key for **correct intonation**.

12

A Major:

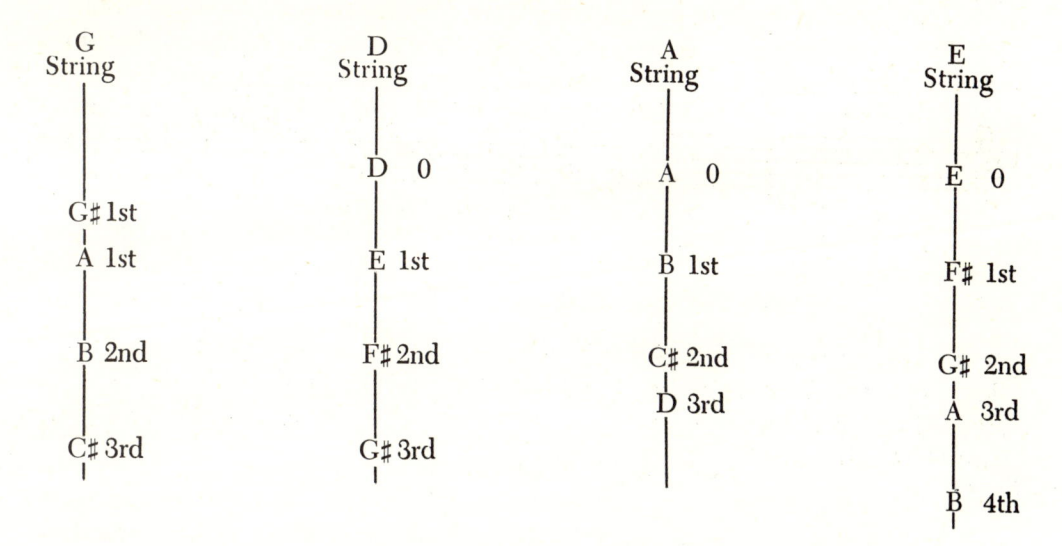

```
G String        D String        A String        E String

                D  0            A  0            E  0
G♯ 1st
A  1st          E  1st          B  1st          F♯ 1st

B  2nd          F♯ 2nd          C♯ 2nd          G♯ 2nd
                                D  3rd          A  3rd
C♯ 3rd          G♯ 3rd
                                                B  4th
```

Key of C:

G String | D String | A String | E String

0 1 2 3   0 1 2 3   0 1 2 3   0 1 2 3 4

The only new notes in this key are the F's. On the E string, the first finger is placed close to the nut.

C Major:

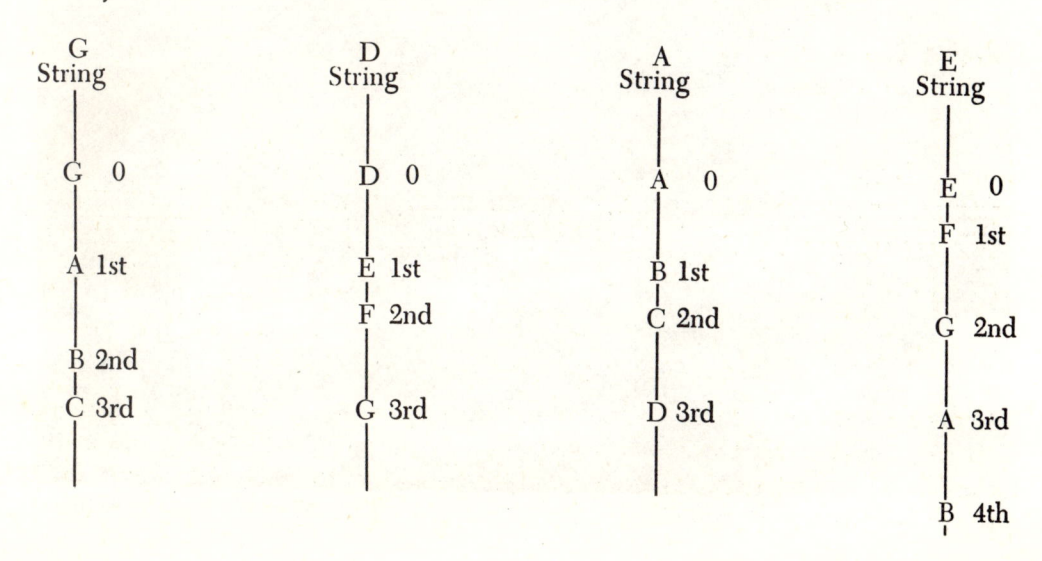

```
G String        D String        A String        E String

G  0            D  0            A  0            E  0
                                                F  1st
A  1st          E  1st          B  1st
                F  2nd          C  2nd          G  2nd
B  2nd
C  3rd          G  3rd          D  3rd          A  3rd

                                                B  4th
```

13

Of the four keys, D is probably the easiest to play. There are countless fine fiddle tunes in this key. Perhaps the most common of all and certainly one of the best is "Soldier's Joy." It is a wonder that never seems to lose its vitality though it has been played for centuries. Robert Burns set some verse to the tune in his *Merry Muses of Caledonia* and there are even older published versions. In the United States it has also been known as *The King's Head* and *Rock the Cradle, Lucy*. Here is a simple setting of the tune which gives its essential melody.

Accomplished fiddlers will generally add more notes to this tune. Once you have learned it by heart and have whistled the tune for a while, you will probably hear more notes in your head that you will want to fit into your version. Added notes are the spice that brings out the flavor and richness of a fiddle tune. But they must be selected with great care. Too often a city bred or otherwise inexperienced fiddler who wants to impress the "simple country folk" will play a tune with too many indiscriminately chosen notes. This only succeeds in betraying bad taste and ignorance of good fiddling. The most important thing in fiddling is always the feeling—the flow of the rhythm. Play *Soldier's Joy* over and over as simply as you can until you are comfortable enough to feel the lilting of the beat. Don't worry about making mistakes. Just keep going until you don't have to think about the rhythm.

The first accomplishment is control of that subtle lilt. If you have recordings of Uncle Charlie Higgins or Frank George, play them until they wear out. Both men possess an almost unerring sense of phrasing. As you immerse yourself in the flow of *Soldier's Joy*, you will naturally find yourself playing slight variations in the phrasing of the notes, little changes that keep the tune lively. This is a sign that you are beginning to fiddle. Don't try to figure it out. You must learn to feel the beat. You will remember phrasing that you like and want to play again. Let your feeling for the rhythm be your first concern. Later, you can start adding notes.

Here are some simple versions of tunes that you may enjoy playing. I recommend that you stick with these for a while. But also play any tunes or songs that you like by ear on your fiddle.

Wade Ward and Charlie Higgins

Soldier's Joy

Shortenin' Bread

Ida Red

Old Joe Clark

DOUBLE STOPS

Probably the most common means of embellishing a fiddle tune is the use of double stops, the sounding of two strings at once. Every Southern Appalachian fiddler I have heard employs some form of double-noting, as it is commonly called. Musicologists who have studied ancient Celtic dance music are in general agreement that much of the style and repertory of the Celtic fiddlers can be traced to the influence of the bagpipes. In highland bagpipe music, one or two notes, called drones, are sounded continuously throughout the playing of a piece in addition to the notes of the melody.

The use of drones has been easily adapted to the fiddle by means of the flattened bridge which allows fiddlers to finger the notes of the melody on one string while simultaneously sounding an adjacent open string. Drones are the simplest form of double-noting. Unlike the bagpipes, however, where the drones sound continuously on the first and fifth tones of the scale regardless of the melody notes being played, the fiddle requires greater ingenuity and allows for more variety in the use of drones. Since fiddle tunes usually require fingering on more than one string, the open string available for sounding a drone will vary throughout most tunes. Also, since drones sound best on the first and fifth tones of the scale, the effectiveness of open strings as drones is further limited by the key in which a tune is played.

When the fiddle is played in standard tuning (GDAE), drones work best in the keys of A, D, and G. For a tune like *Shortenin' Bread,* for example, either the open A or E string can be employed almost constantly as a drone. Try keeping your bow on both the A and E strings throughout as you play this tune. There are many simple dance tunes in the key of A which can be double-noted this way.

Many of the older fiddlers retune their fiddles in order to make more open strings available as drones. You can play *Shortenin' Bread* with your G and D strings tuned up to A and E. Now your fiddle is tuned AEAE and you can finger the tune the same way on the two low strings as you did on the two high strings. You can now play the tune an octave lower with the same drone effect. And you can also use the two middle strings together as drones in this tuning.

When playing in the key of D with the fiddle tuned GDAE, you will have to be more careful about allowing your bow to strike open strings. Basically, you are limited to the two middle strings, D and A. Try applying a drone technique to *Soldier's Joy.*

In the key of G, some good use can be made of the two lowest strings, G and D. Many of the best tunes in this key require extensive noting on the high E string which cannot be accompanied by a drone as the open A string sounds discordant in this key. But *Ida Red* can be played very effectively with drones. Here the D string will work as a drone almost throughout the tune. When you have to finger on the D string, let your box strike the low G string and you will realize the possibilities for drones in this key.

The use of drones is greatly restricted in the key of C. Of the open strings, only the low G string sounds a pitch which is effective as a drone. Since much of the fingering of tunes in this key is done on the high strings, the G string is rarely available as a drone.

Because of the inherent limitations of playing drones on the fiddle and the comparative ease with which fingering can be applied simultaneously on adjacent strings, fiddlers have developed more sophisticated forms of double-noting in addition to the simple use of drones. These more complex forms of double-noting constitute a system of fingering positions analogous to the chord positions utilized by guitar and banjo players. Knowledge of these positions and their mastery provide a fiddler with the means for greater harmonic enrichment and emphasis.

Here are the basic double-note fingering position:

0-1 Position

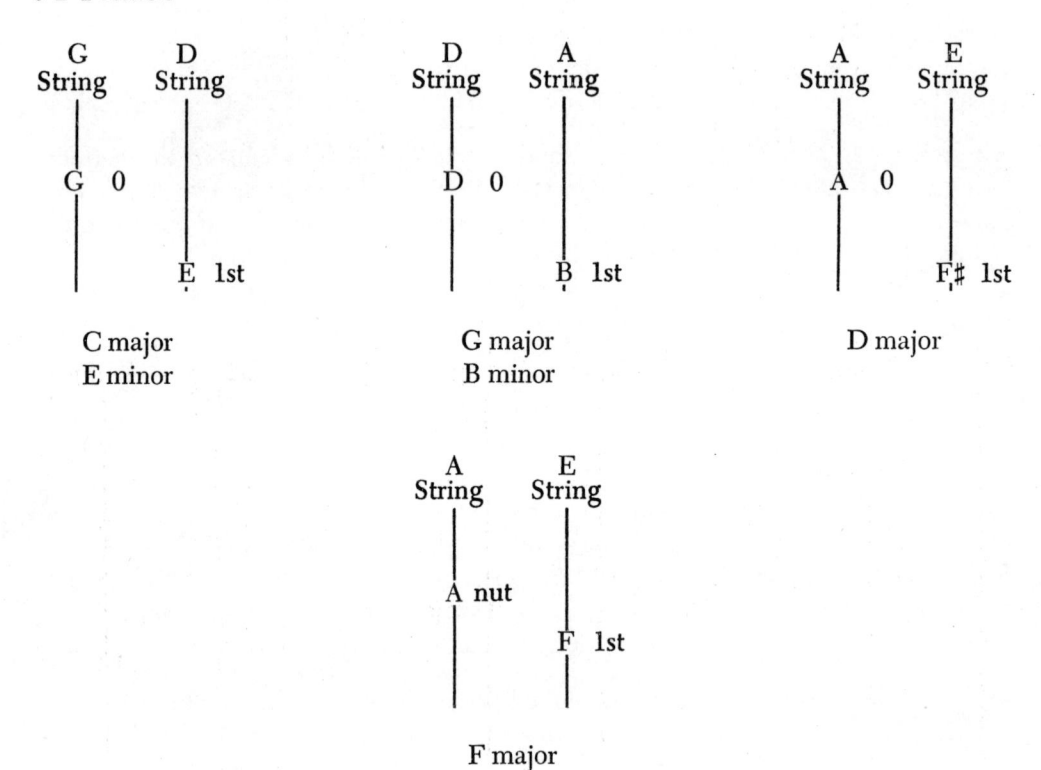

```
G        D              D        A              A        E
String   String         String   String         String   String
|        |              |        |              |        |
G  0                    D  0                    A  0
|        |              |        |              |        |
|        E  1st         |        B  1st         |        F♯ 1st
|        |              |        |              |        |

C major                 G major                 D major
E minor                 B minor
```

```
        A        E
        String   String
        |        |
        A nut
        |        |
        |        F  1st
        |        |

        F major
```

3-1 Position

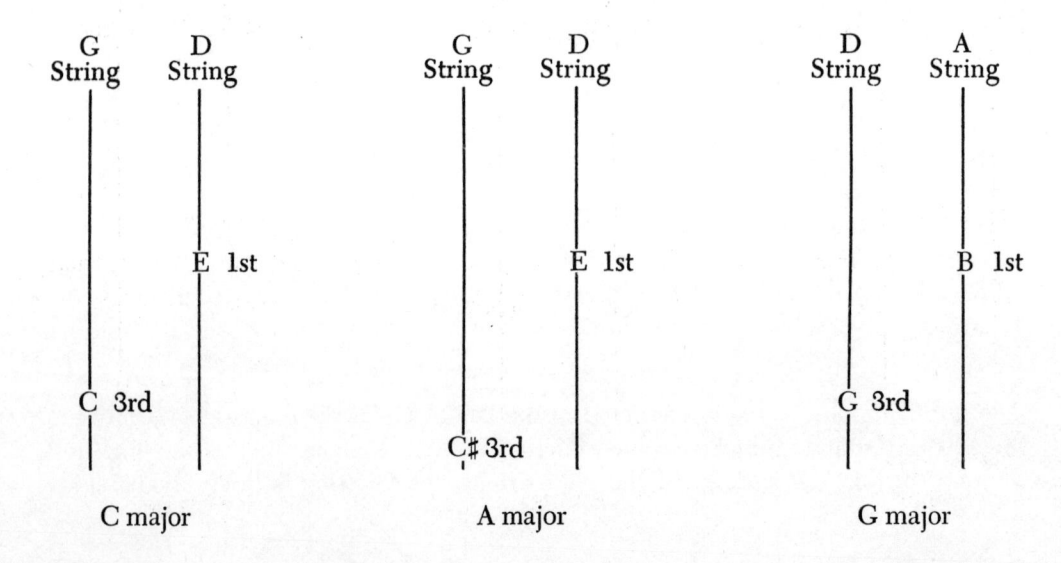

```
G        D              G        D              D        A
String   String         String   String         String   String
|        |              |        |              |        |
|        E  1st         |        E  1st         |        B  1st
|        |              |        |              |        |
C  3rd                  |        |              G  3rd
|        |              C♯ 3rd                  |        |
|        |              |        |              |        |

C major                 A major                 G major
```

18

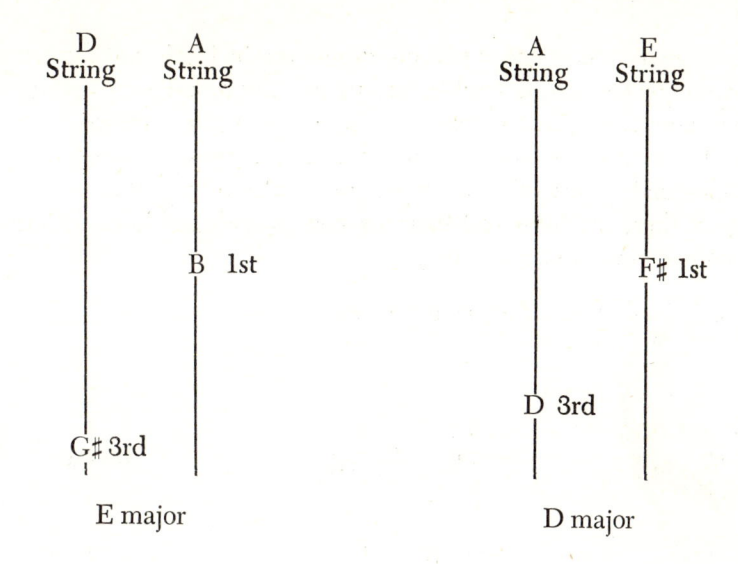

```
   D        A              A        E
 String   String          String  String
   |        |               |       |
   |        |               |       |
   |      B 1st             |     F♯ 1st
   |        |               |       |
   |        |               |       |
   |        |             D 3rd     |
 G♯ 3rd     |               |       |
   |        |               |       |

     E major                  D major
```

1-2 Position

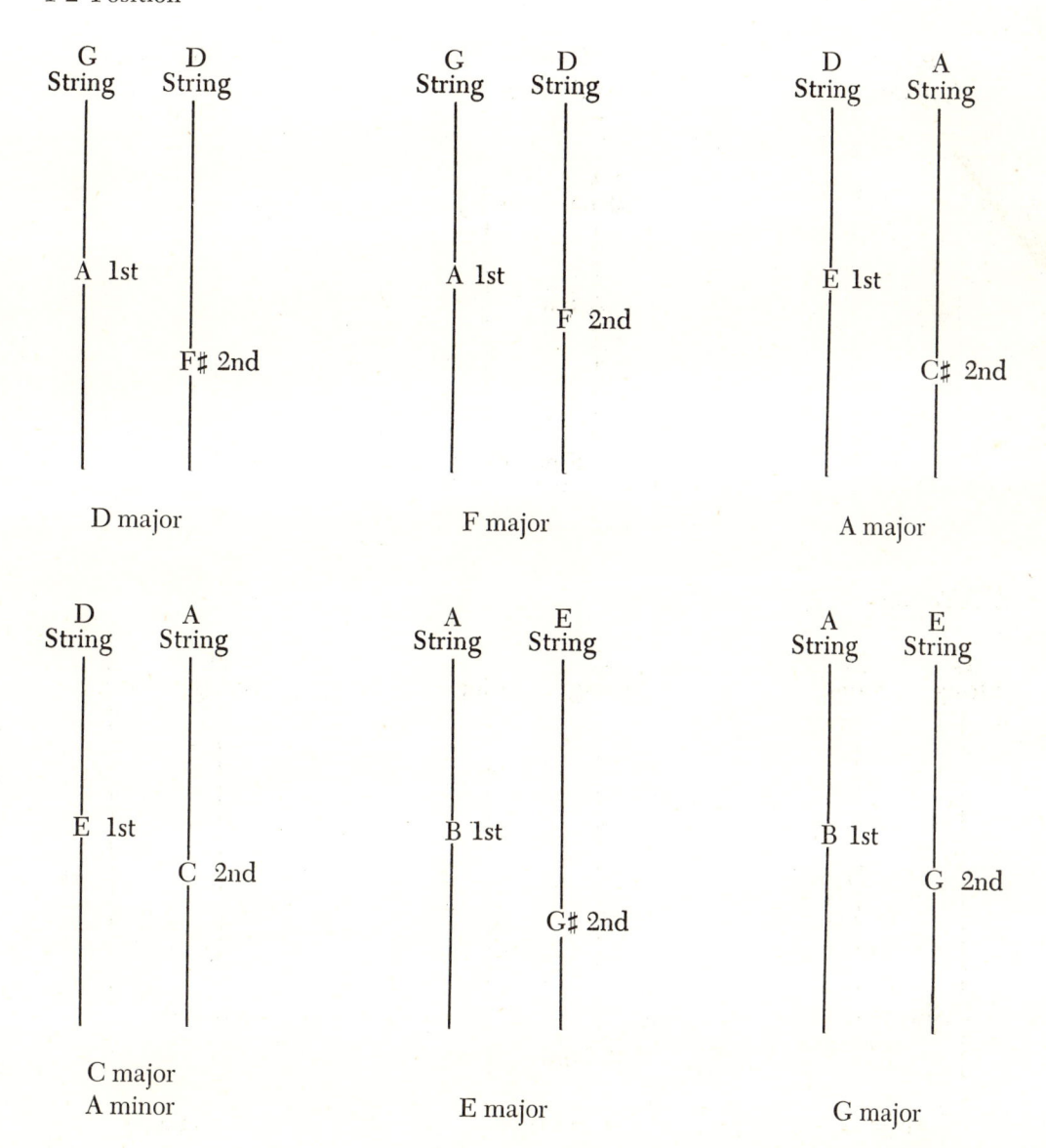

```
  G       D           G       D           D       A
String  String      String  String      String  String
  |       |           |       |           |       |
  |       |           |       |           |       |
A 1st     |         A 1st     |         E 1st     |
  |       |           |       |           |       |
  |     F♯ 2nd        |     F 2nd         |     C♯ 2nd
  |       |           |       |           |       |

   D major             F major             A major


  D       A           A       E           A       E
String  String      String  String      String  String
  |       |           |       |           |       |
  |       |           |       |           |       |
E 1st     |         B 1st     |         B 1st     |
  |     C 2nd          |       |           |     G 2nd
  |       |           |     G♯ 2nd         |       |

   C major             E major             G major
   A minor
```

1-0 Position

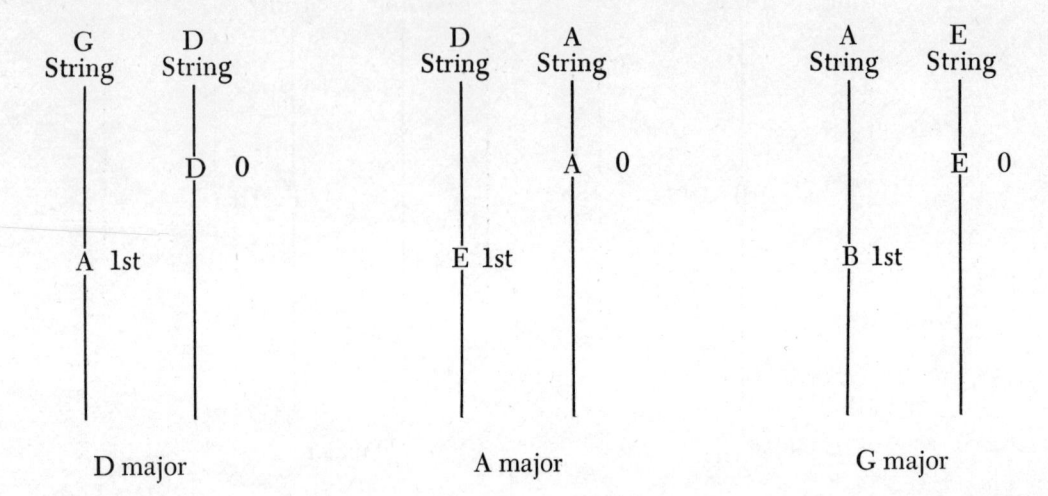

| G String / D String — D 0, A 1st — **D major** | D String / A String — A 0, E 1st — **A major** | A String / E String — E 0, B 1st — **G major** |

2-0 Position

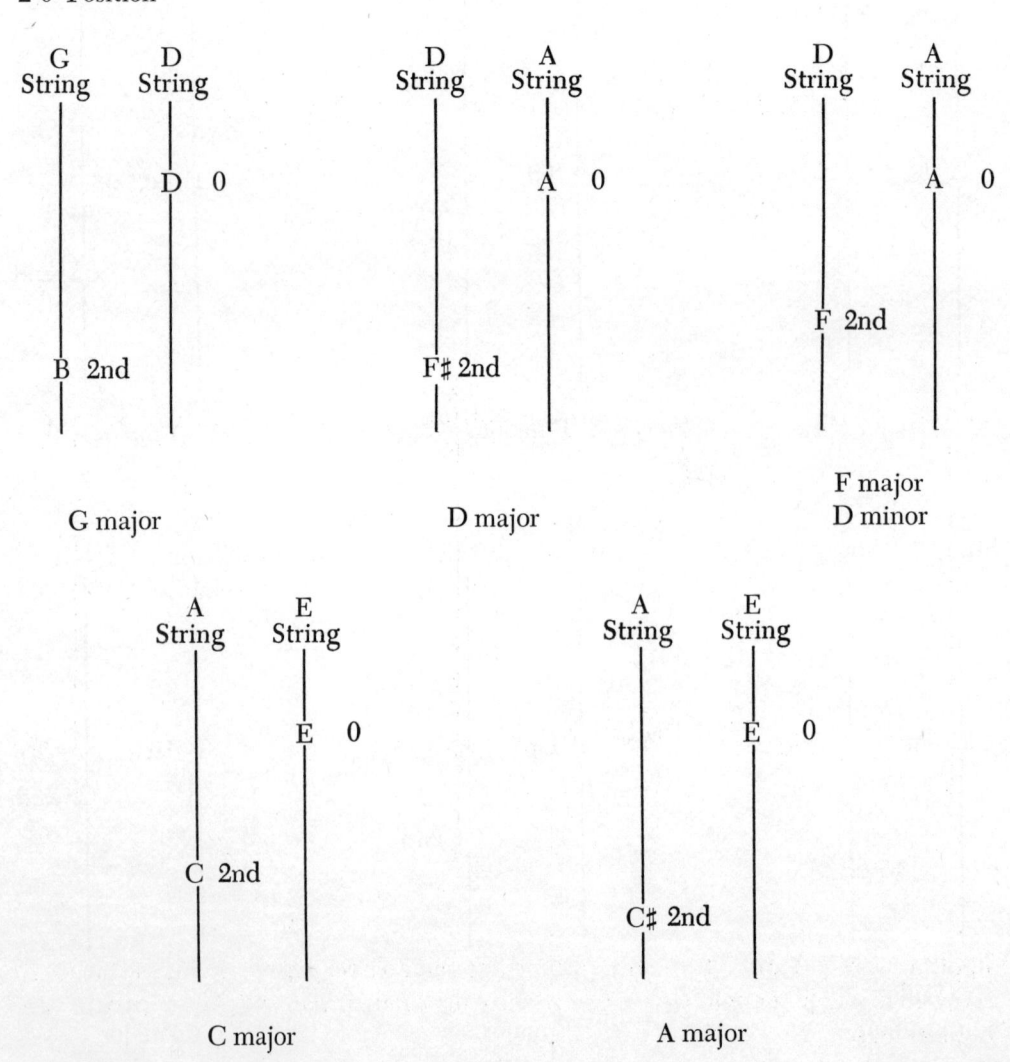

| G String / D String — D 0, B 2nd — **G major** | D String / A String — A 0, F♯ 2nd — **D major** | D String / A String — A 0, F 2nd — **F major / D minor** |

| A String / E String — E 0, C 2nd — **C major** | A String / E String — E 0, C♯ 2nd — **A major** |

1-1 Position

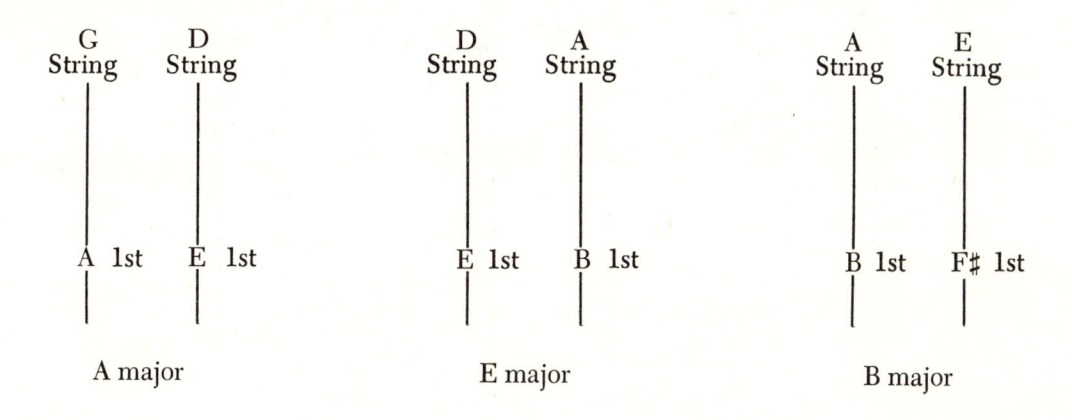

G String	D String		D String	A String		A String	E String
A 1st	E 1st		E 1st	B 1st		B 1st	F♯ 1st
A major			E major			B major	

2-2 Position

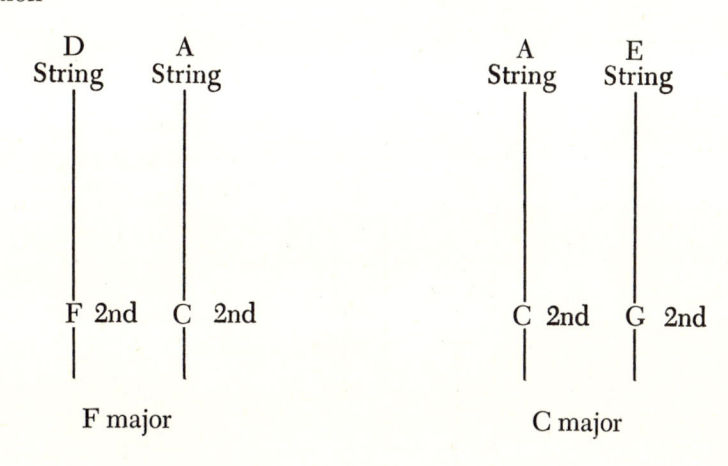

D String	A String		A String	E String
F 2nd	C 2nd		C 2nd	G 2nd
F major			C major	

3-3 Position

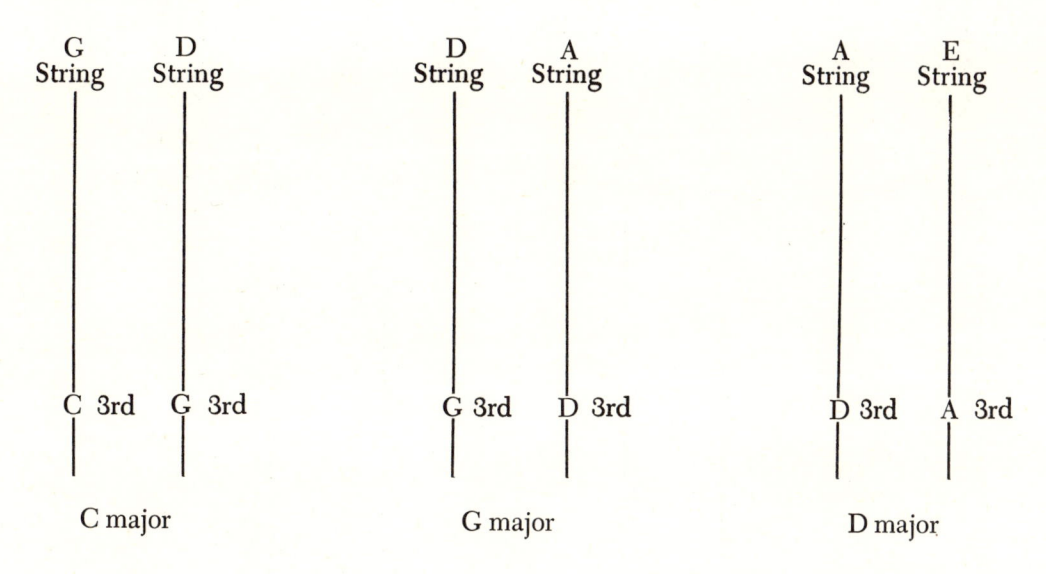

G String	D String		D String	A String		A String	E String
C 3rd	G 3rd		G 3rd	D 3rd		D 3rd	A 3rd
C major			G major			D major	

Positions 1-1, 2-2 and 3-3 require placing the same finger on two strings at once. In these cases the finger will have to be slightly bent rather than arched in order to note both strings.

2-3 Position

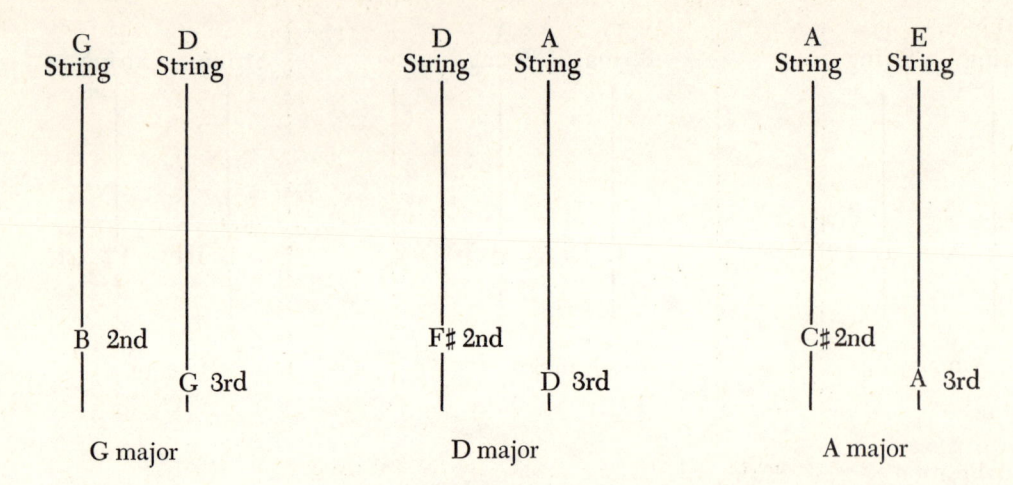

G String	D String		D String	A String		A String	E String
B 2nd			F# 2nd			C# 2nd	
	G 3rd			D 3rd			A 3rd
G major			D major			A major	

3-2 Position

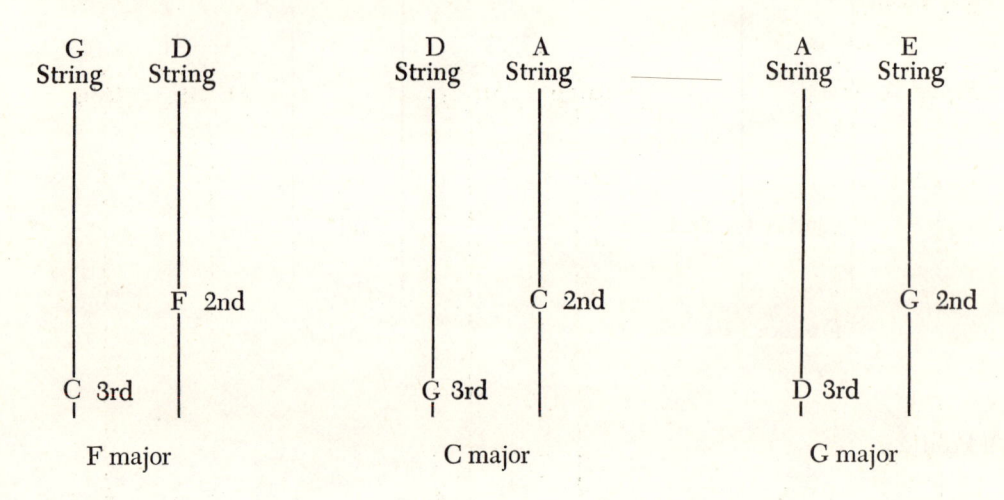

G String	D String		D String	A String		A String	E String
	F 2nd			C 2nd			G 2nd
C 3rd			G 3rd			D 3rd	
F major			C major			G major	

4-2 Position

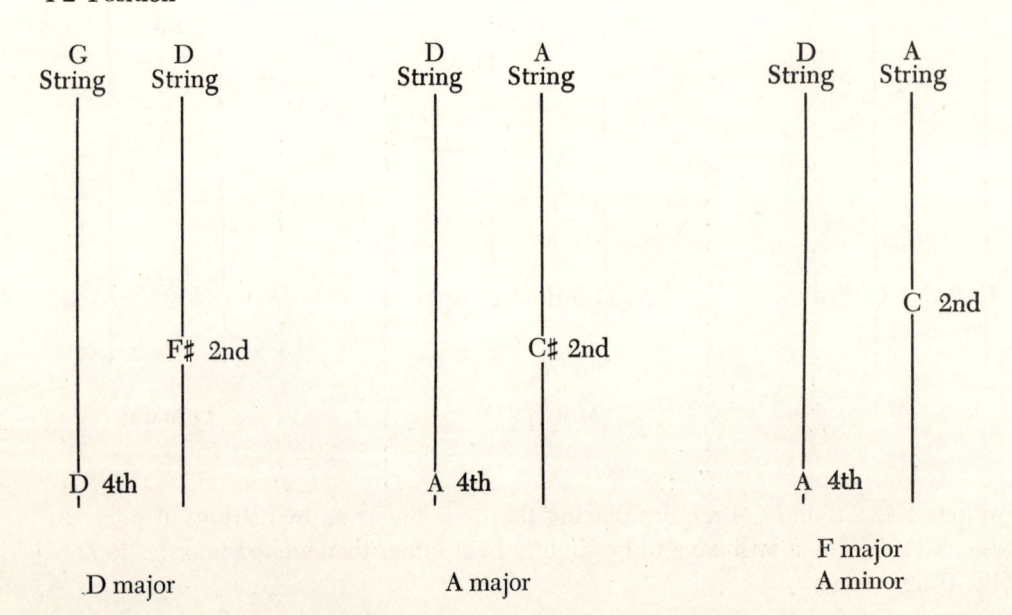

G String	D String		D String	A String		D String	A String
	F# 2nd			C# 2nd			C 2nd
D 4th			A 4th			A 4th	
D major			A major			F major / A minor	

22

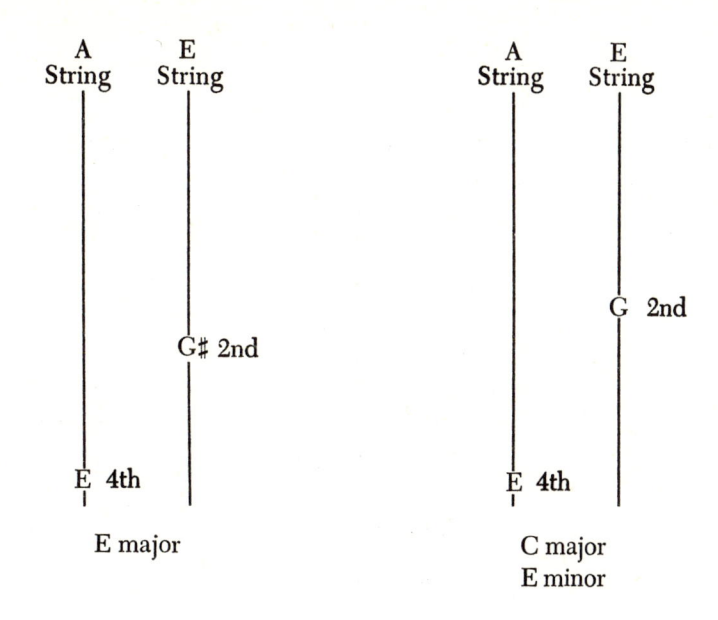

A E	A E
String String	String String
G♯ 2nd	G 2nd
E 4th	E 4th
E major	C major
	E minor

3-4 Position

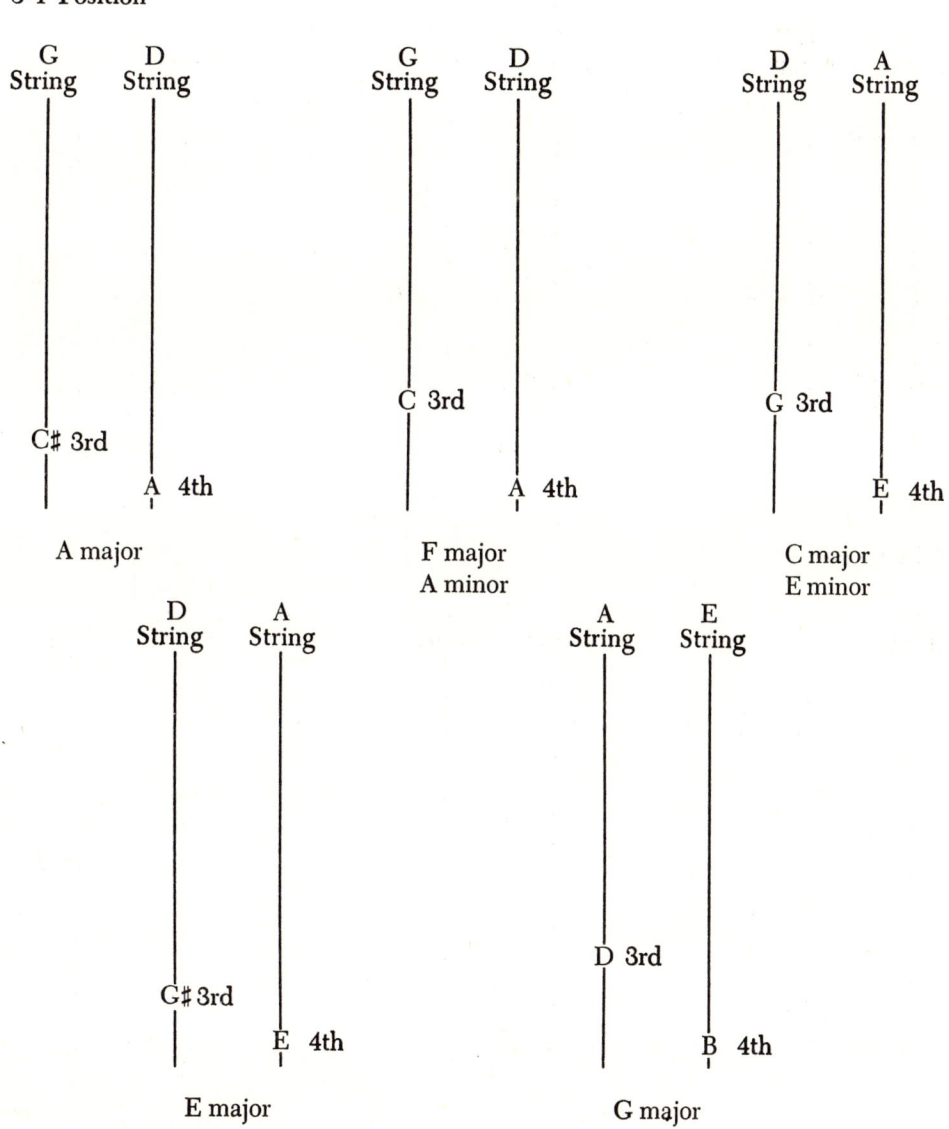

G D	G D	D A
String String	String String	String String
	C 3rd	G 3rd
C♯ 3rd		
A 4th	A 4th	E 4th
A major	F major	C major
	A minor	E minor

D A	A E
String String	String String
	D 3rd
G♯ 3rd	
E 4th	B 4th
E major	G major

23

4-3 Position

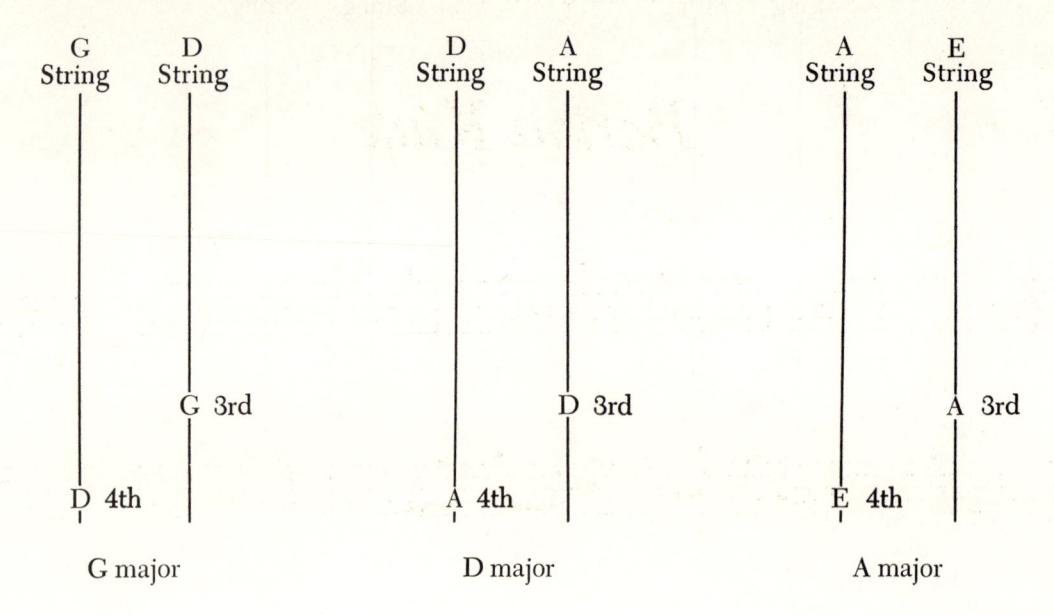

G String	D String		D String	A String		A String	E String
	G 3rd			D 3rd			A 3rd
D 4th			A 4th			E 4th	
G major			D major			A major	

2-1 Position

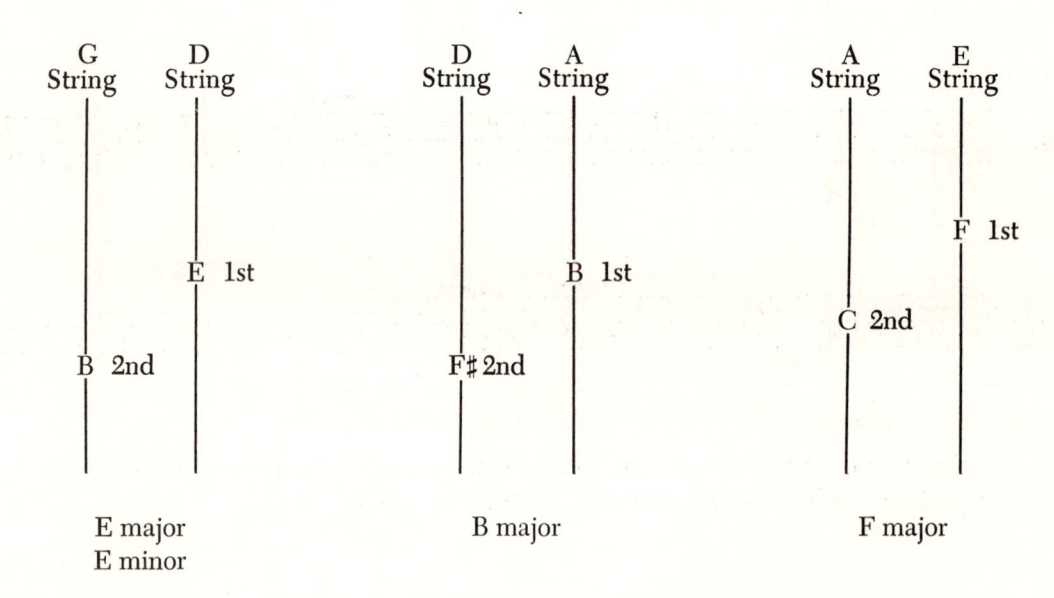

G String	D String		D String	A String		A String	E String
	E 1st			B 1st			F 1st
B 2nd			F♯ 2nd			C 2nd	
E major			B major			F major	
E minor							

This chart may seem rather imposing at first glance. However, the harmonic accompaniment to traditional fiddle tunes is usually limited to not more than three chords. So you will generally have to choose from the double-note positions which fit these chords when working out a version of any particular tune. Tunes in the key of G are generally limited harmonically to the chords G, D, and C. In the key of A, you will usually use the chords A, E, and D. The key of D relies on the chords D, A, and G. And the key of C uses the chords C, G, and F and frequently A minor.

It should always be kept in mind that double-noting is a technique of emphasis and enrichment. Use double-note positions only when they can fit into your playing without distracting from the melody. As you play a tune you will discover places where a double stop will fit naturally. This is always the best criterion for its use.

Barlow Knife is a fine old tune that really lends itself to double-noting. First, let's look at a simple transcription of the melody:

Barlow Knife

Practice this unadorned version until the bowing becomes easy and natural. Now let's look at *Barlow Knife* with drones and double stops added.

Barlow Knife

Under the staff you will find the double-note fingering written. You should not have to alter the bowing pattern you developed when playing the simplified version. Just allow your bow to strike the additional string and note it with the required finger where necessary.

Here is another good tune that is easy to play with double-noting.

Angeline

And here is *Angeline* with double-notes added.

Angeline

Now let's look at the way double-noting can be applied to a tune in the key of A.

Dinah

Now a version with double-noting.

Dinah

Remember, these transcriptions are merely examples of one way a tune can be played. In this chapter the transcriptions are meant to illustrate methods of double-noting in playing fiddle tunes. You need not feel bound to play any tune exactly the way it is written out here. Nor will you be happy if you can only play a tune one way over and over. Learn a version of each tune that consists of all the essential notes of the melody and play it with a nice bouncing flow. Once you are sure of a basic way to play a tune you can start working out more involved ways of playing it.

The transcriptions of the following three tunes give only their basic melodies. Try to work out versions for yourself.

29

West Fork Girls is a really fine tune that fiddlers love to play around Gilmer County, West Virginia. At the West Virginia State Folk Festival I have seen as many as seven or eight fiddlers enjoying this tune together.

West Fork Girls

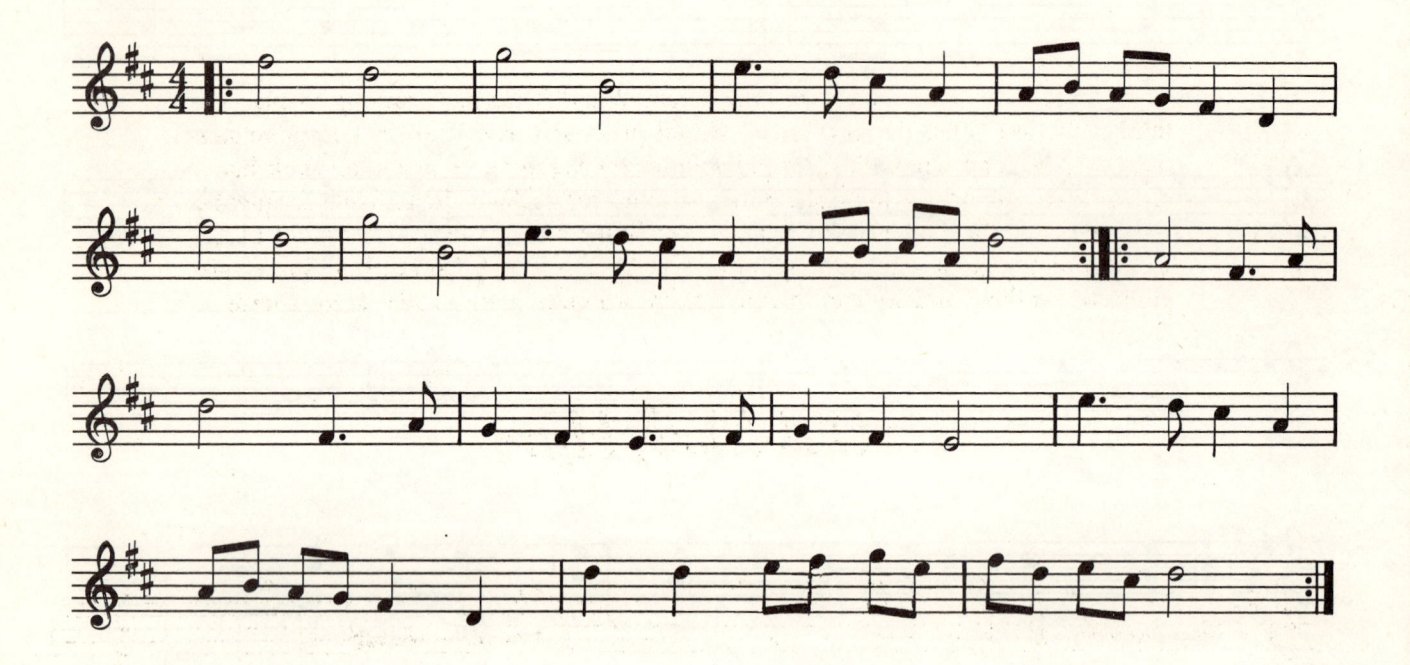

Boogerman is most common in North Carolina. However, it is a simple example of a type of tune in the key of G which is found throughout the Appalachians. The first part of the tune is in the key of G. But the second part goes to E minor, or E major as it is often harmonized by mountain guitarists. Other examples of tunes with this progression are *Stony Point* and *Teetotaller* which we will be looking at later.

Boogerman

Old Molly Hare is one of my favorite tunes. When I was first learning to play the fiddle, this was often the first tune I would play each day. With its deceptive simplicity, spirit, and almost infinite possibilities for variation, it seems to work like a charm that puts one in the right frame of mind for fiddling. It has been frequently recorded, but the best version I have ever heard was on an old recording in the Library of Congress with fiddling and vocal by Uncle Eck Dunford of Galax, Virginia. In Scotland and Ireland this tune is known quite aptly as *The Fairy Dance*.

Old Molly Hare

MODAL TUNES

Modal tunes are a type of melody common in the Southern Appalachians which uses a scale that is neither major nor minor. I like to call them A to G tunes since they are usually based on a harmonic progression which moves from A (either major or minor) to G and back to A. This progression, so deceptively simple, has nevertheless proved vital enough to provide a basis for many of the oldest and most distinctive Southern Appalachian fiddle tunes.

Although played in all parts of the mountains, modal tunes are most plentiful in the areas of West Virginia and eastern Kentucky. In these states it is still possible to meet an old fiddler who can play modal tunes for hours on end without repeating himself. Modal tunes are for the white mountaineer what the blues are for the rural southern Black. These tunes seem to naturally express the temperament of the mountaineer in his rugged and isolated environment. Perhaps this is why they still remain most common in those parts of the mountains which have been least affected by the synthetic culture of our times.

Basically, modal tunes hark back to the old Highland Scottish bagpipe music. The Scottish bagpipe chanter sounds a pitch just slightly sharper than G♯ in the key of A. The pipes cannot play a G♯ which ordinarily helps to establish both the major and minor tonalities of the key of A. Consequently, highland pipe music contains a great variety of A to G tunes in a mode which is called the *double tonic*.

Probably, settlers of Scotch-Irish descent brought this modality with them to the Southern Appalachians where it nurtured the beautiful modal fiddle tunes which are by now distinctly American.

Oscar Wright

Ducks on the Pond is a modal tune I first heard played at The Old Fiddler's Convention at Galax, Virginia. Standing around the circle where Frank George was playing, I noticed a gentle man of about 60 years of age who was intently listening to the music. I had the feeling that he was a fiddler but had never seen him playing in public. Later that evening, Frank George, knowing that I liked modal tunes, told me that I had better hear Oscar Wright play *Ducks on the Pond*. We walked over to where this same gentleman was standing off beyond the noise and press of the crowd. He was at first reluctant to play but after Frank got me to make a few attempts at the *Red Haired Boy,* I handed Oscar Wright my fiddle and we persuaded him to play *Ducks on the Pond*. It went something like this:

Ducks on the Pond

Another of Oscar's fine tunes which was learned from the legendary Henry Reed is *Kitchen Girl*.

Kitchen Girl

Uncle Charlie Higgins, the great Galax, Virginia fiddler played only a few A to G tunes. But his version of *June Apple* is the best I have ever heard. The version below is derived from the playing of Uncle Charlie.

June Apple

Uncle Charlie played for many years with Wade Ward, perhaps the finest Virginia clawhammer banjo player of his generation. A recording of them playing *June Apple* has been issued by Alan Lomax on the Prestige/International "Southern Journey Series." Another of their tunes was *Cluck Old Hen*, a favorite of fiddle and banjo players throughout the Appalachians.

Cluck Old Hen

Franklin George, like Uncle Charlie Higgins, tends to play more intricate tunes than the average fiddler. *The 28th of January* is a very interesting and unusual "A to G" tune with rather difficult fingering. I learned this tune from the playing of Frank George and Dave Milefsky.

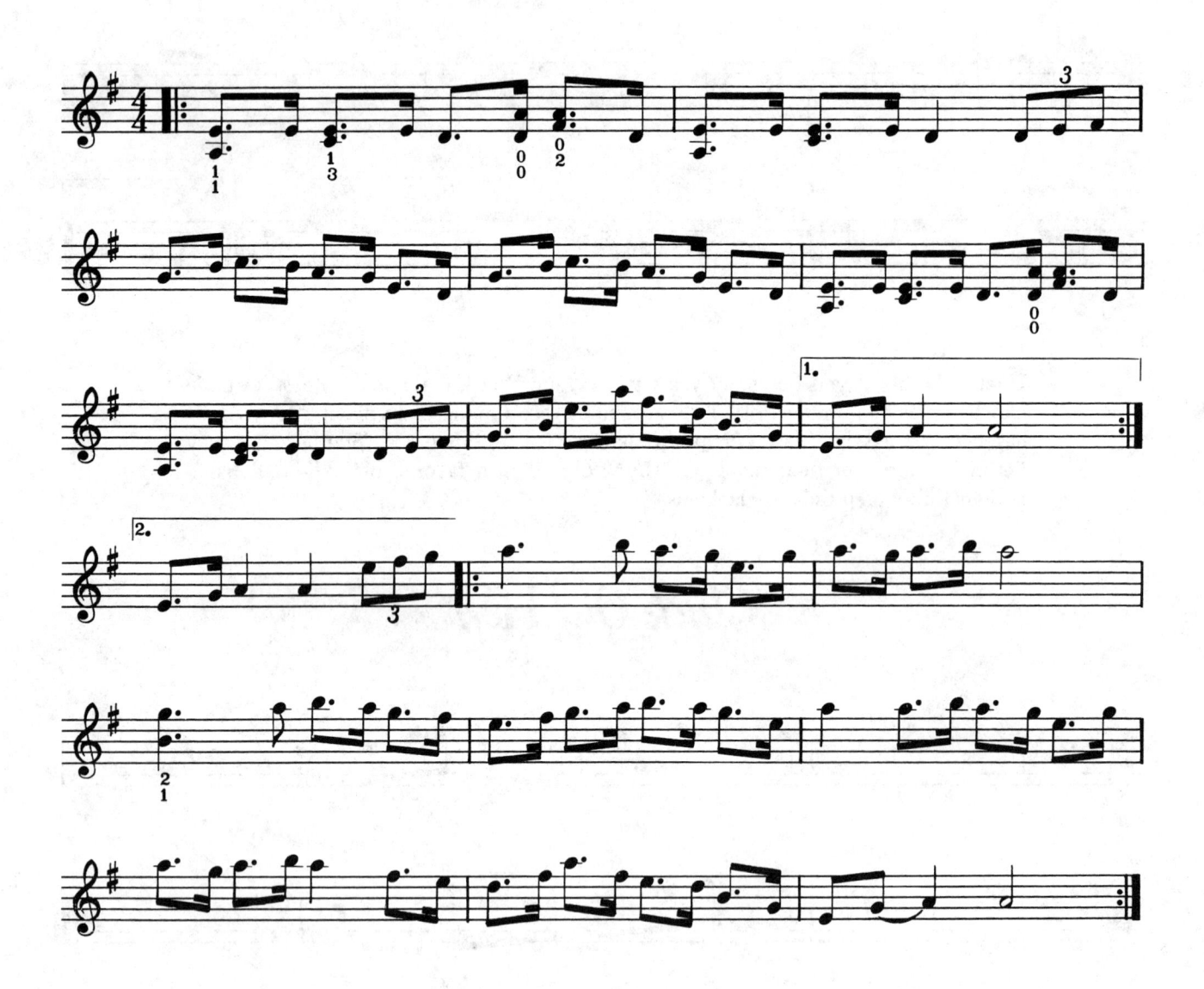

28th of January

Salt River is a tune I learned from Frank George. This is essentially the same tune which Bill Monroe has popularized among the bluegrassers as *Salt Creek*. However, it is a much older tune and played by fiddlers in various parts of the country. You can hear many interesting versions of this tune played in West Virginia. Frank's version retains the older elements of the melody in a more developed form than the popular bluegrass versions.

Salt River

The Kentucky mountains, even more remote than West Virginia, are rich with old fiddlers and archaic modal tunes. *Lonesome John* comes close to epitomizing the Kentucky mountain fiddler. Here is a version derived from the playing of Fiddlin' Sam Kelly of W. Liberty, Kentucky.

Lonesome John

I learned *Cold Frosty Morning* from Joel Shimberg of Arlington, Virginia. It is a modal tune in the same vein as *Ducks on the Pond* and *Kitchen Girl*. All three were collected from Henry Reed by Alan Jabbour, a fine fiddler and Director of the Archives of American Folk Song at the Library of Congress.

Cold Frosty Morning

Alan Jabbour played the following tune back in 1965. He had learned it from Henry Reed but, at that time, did not know its name. Frank George likened it to one his teacher, Jim Farthing, had called *Fire on the Mountain*. I have heard several other versions in West Virginia, some with words and called *West Virginia Girls*.

West Virginia Girls

French Carpenter, Roscoe and Phoeba Parsons

Of all the fiddlers I have ever heard, French Carpenter of Clay County, West Virginia played the most beautiful and rare modal tunes. A recording of his playing has been issued by Kanawha Records. Here is a version of his tune, *Yew Piney Mountain*.

Yew Piney Mountain

When French played this tune he had his fiddle tuned AEAE. If you retune, you will find it easier to finger the low notes as the fourth finger will no longer be required on the D string. The AEAE tuning also allows for greater use of drones on the low strings.

BREAKDOWNS IN D

The staple element of most Appalachian fiddlers' repertories is the rich collection of breakdowns, the brisk tunes played for most Appalachian dances. Many of these tunes are very old and can be traced to the dance tunes known as "reels" in the British Isles. For the most part the exact origins of the tunes are obscure. It is common to hear a fiddler state that a tune has been played in his part of the country as long as any one can remember. Often an older fiddler will be credited with popularizing a tune in his area. But only occasionally is it said that a tune was composed or "made" by a particular individual. Sometimes, new tunes do appear. Especially in the last fifty years, tunes which have been put together by commercial fiddlers on phonograph records have been accepted into traditional repertories. But basically fiddlers tend to be conservative. The playing of breakdowns in the Southern Appalachians is an expression of joy. New tunes or ways of playing them are only of interest to fiddlers in so far as they augment the existing means of expressing this feeling. In recent years the increasing popularity of fiddlers' contests has encouraged an element of competitiveness among musicians, but still the spirit of the old music lives on. Fiddlers at their best play for the joy of the music which makes people feel good and want to dance. In practice this means not playing too fast and not imposing on a tune notes which merely demonstrate technical facility and are not consistent with the tune's character.

Fiddlers genuinely love the tunes they play. Each tune seems to possess a particular character or singular way of expressing the joyous quality that is common to all Appalachian dance music. I have always looked upon fiddlers as people who in at least one area of their lives were a type of Western wise man. Their tunes were like incantations, a form of ancient wisdom that induced high feeling. Of all the best Appalachian fiddlers that I have heard, despite the individual differences, their styles all had one thing in common: the feeling of the music was always primary. Whatever technical facility they possessed, and many had accomplished mastery of their instruments, their techniques were always developed to better express the feeling of their music.

The tunes that follow in this chapter are breakdowns in the key of D. They are transcribed in most cases in versions that I play and which are based on the "lessons" I have taken from traditional fiddlers. Occasionally, I have simplified the transcriptions so as not to introduce anything too technically difficult. None of the transcriptions are meant for actual performances. In no instance have I included every variation that I know or might play on a given occasion. Each transcription does give at least what I believe to be the essential character of the tune and, in many cases, suggestions toward how the tune can be explored.

You can learn tunes from this book. But you should keep in mind that real development as a fiddler requires listening to the playing of other fiddlers. How you ultimately play a tune will be determined by your own technical ability and taste.

Forked Deer

Alternate Low Part

Forked Deer is a very popular tune in the Appalachians. There are at least four good recorded versions. Frank George and John Summers, French Carpenter, Charlie Bowman, and Taylor's Kentucky Boys have made recordings which will be of interest to any fiddler. The transcription above derives mainly from Frank George's playing, but the first low part is based on a version I heard John Rector fiddle with Wade Ward.

Arkansas Traveller

Everyone has heard this tune. But notice how in the version above, learned from Frank George, the notes of the high part seem particularly chosen to gracefully complement the lilting beat. As in all of these tunes, I would advise that you first practice playing slowly, bowing out each of the notes with short strokes in the upper third of your bow. When you have gained control of your left hand and do not have to think about where to place your fingers, you can begin concentrating on fitting your bowing to the bouncing rhythm implied by the notes.

Soldier's Joy

Charlie Higgins' High Variation

Here is a more developed version of *Soldier's Joy* than the one in chapter one. Charlie Higgins' variation on the high part is one of many fiddlers play.

Fortune

This is essentially Charlie Higgins' version. *Fortune* is most popular around Galax, Va. It is also sometimes known as *"Once I had A Fortune"* and has been recorded as such for the Library of Congress by the Bogtrotters with Crockett Ward on fiddle, Wade Ward on banjo, and vocal and guitar by Fields Ward.

Backstep Cindy

This is another Galax area tune. It is also known as *Step Back Cindy* and sometimes as *Backstep*. Several versions have been recorded on County Records. The version above comes from Charlie Higgins and contains a more developed melody than other versions I have heard.

Ragtime Annie is almost certainly a native American dance tune, possibly less than 100 years old. The transcribed version is one that I have put together. It has been influenced in different ways by fiddlers as diverse as Frank George, Soloman and Hughes, and Clark Kessinger. The first part begins by sliding your second finger up from F to F♯ on the D string. You will find it easier to do the crossbowing, i.e. alternately playing on the A and D strings as in measure two, if you begin with an up-bow on the A string. This means starting at the tip of the bow and pushing up. For the next note you pull your bow across the D string and towards the frog. Then return to the A string with an up-bow and continue alternating up and down-bows as you need to cross strings. Crossbowing is a technique that is used in many good tunes like *Leatherbreeches* and *Durang's Hornpipe*.

Ragtime Annie

Clark Kessinger and his band

This is another of Charlie Higgins' versions. This is the tune that served as melody for the song, *The Battle of New Orleans*. It is a good example of the way a fine fiddler can make a very popular tune even more beautiful and interesting.

Eighth of January

This is a version I put together of a terrific fiddle and banjo tune. It is one of those intriguingly simple pieces like *Old Molly Hare* which can be varied just slightly in so many different ways. Yet each time only a single note is changed, new life is instilled into your playing.

Blackeyed Susan

Frank George

Dusty Miller

This is an unusual tune that Frank George plays. A totally unrelated fiddle tune of the same name is played in the key of A. I learned this tune from Armin Barnett of Charlottesville, Va.

Quince Dillon's High D Tune

This is one of Henry Reed's tunes collected by Alan Jabbour. Henry Reed didn't remember its name but mentioned it as one of the tunes he learned from a fife player, named Quincy Dillon. Many of the young fiddlers like Bill Hicks, Armin Barnett, and Dave Milefsky are now playing this tune, calling it *Quince Dillon's High D Tune*. To play that high D, slide your left hand up the neck, your first finger fingers A on the E string, i.e., your first finger must move up to where your third finger would ordinarily be. With your hand in this position you should be able to reach the high D with your fourth finger.

G TUNES

Tunes in the key of G are more difficult to play than those in the key of D. This is because more fingering is required when continually playing on the A and E strings. In the key of G, these strings when played open do not sound the most important notes of the scale, G and D. Consequently, you cannot rely on them so much for intonation but must learn to place your third finger accurately on the D string and your second finger on the E if you are to play them in tune. The precise positioning of the second finger on the A string for the note C is also sometimes a problem for fiddlers who play more often in the keys of D and A. Also, you cannot use your open A and E strings so often for drones in this key but must place your fingers accurately on two strings at once for double-note effects in this key.

Alan Jabbour and Sherman Hammons

This is a fairly simple G tune that I learned from Henry Reed.

Red Fox

This is another Henry Reed tune. I first heard it played by Dave Milefsky. It is very similar to a tune Uncle Dave Macon and the Fruit Jar Drinkers recorded in the key of D, entitled *Jordan Is A Hard Road To Travel, I Believe*. A closer variant is the recording of *Johnson City Rag* by James McCarroll and the Roane County Ramblers.

Jawbone

Cumberland Gap

1st Variation

2nd Variation

A very common tune and many recordings are available. My version is the result of appreciating the playing of Uncle Am Stuart, a Tennessee fiddler who recorded for Vocalion in the 1920's, and Charlie Higgins.

Silly Bill

This tune was recorded by Al Hopkins and the Bucklebusters who hailed from the Galax area. The version above is based more on the playing of Charlie Higgins and Wade Ward.

Blackberry Blossom

Alternate High Part

This version is based on but is not an exact transcription of one of Charlie Higgins' special tunes. Uncle Charlie fiddled until just about his 90th year. Although his playing was declining towards the end, he always seemed capable of playing this difficult piece. In fact, the last few times I saw him, it seemed that *Blackberry Blossom* was the only tune he cared to play. Burnett and Ruttledge recorded the tune in the 1920's.

Stoney Point

This is probably the most common of the G tunes that has an E minor part. French Carpenter recorded a version on his Kanawha album under the title of *Wild Horse*. Another fine version was played by Fiddlin' Powers on a 78 record called the *Old Time Virginia Reel, Part I*. On the record he names the tune *Buck Creek Girls*. Jilson Setters, an old fiddler from Kentucky, called it *Wild Horse at Stoney Point* on his 78 record. Other names are *Pigtown Fling* in the northern states and *Old Dad* in the Galax area. Most versions of this tune contain only two parts, some variant of the first and third printed above. The beautiful and rare middle part in this transcription was learned from Frank George.

Teetotaller

A Kentucky fiddler named Doc Roberts made a 78 record of this tune but called it, *The Devil in Georgia*. I learned this version from Frank George. The tune is also known as *The Temperance Reel*. The sixteenth note figure in the first measure is an Irish ornament on the note G that some Appalachian fiddlers employ. It will become more important when you begin playing hornpipes or if you become interested in Irish fiddling. The four notes should all be executed in one bow stroke. Start the triplet on an up-bow. Play the quarternote, G, with a down-bow. Then play all four sixteenth notes and the following eighth note, G, with an up-bow.

Ebenezer

I originally learned this tune from Frank George and then heard a version fiddled by Kahle Brewer of Galax on an Ernest Stoneman 78 recording called, "West Virginia Highway." Charlie Higgins called the tune, *West Virginia Farewell*. The version above is based on all three.

Sandy River Belle

This is a fairly common tune in the Galax area. This version comes mainly from Frank George and Henry Reed.

Roundtown Girls

This is one of the most common square dance tunes. It is also called *Buffalo Gals* and *Alabama Gals Won't You Come Out Tonight*. The version above is a melodically developed one that I worked out myself after hearing the tune hundreds of times. Frank George and Kahle Brewer have influenced this version most directly.

TUNES IN A AND C

The important thing to remember when playing in the key of A is to get the G#'s in tune. This means positioning your third finger a little higher on the D string than in the keys of G and D and placing your second finger a little higher on the E string than you do when playing in the keys of G and D.

Tommy Jarrell

Brown's Dream

66

This tune goes by many names in the Appalachians including *Pretty Little Miss* and *Little Rabbit*. It is often called *John Brown's Dream* but some fiddlers claim that its original name was *Herve Brown's Dream*. According to this story, the title was shortened to *Brown's Dream* in common usage. Evidently, as the tune circulated, the surname Brown came to be identified with John Brown, the abolitionist, rather than the obscure Herve who may or may not have authored the tune. Fred Cockerham and Tommy Jarrell play versions of this tune with a simpler melody, but with more distinct parts and a lot of double-noting. The Crockett Family recorded a good version on 78 called *Little Rabbit*. But the version above comes mainly from Henry Reed.

Bill Cheatem

Bill Cheatem is a common fiddle tune throughout the Southern part of the United States. The best recorded version I have heard is on a 78 record by the Red Headed Fiddlers, a band from Texas. This transcription is based on their version and also on Henry Reed's.

Boatsman

Boatsman is not strictly speaking a breakdown, but rather an old minstrel tune from the nineteenth century. Frank George recorded it on banjo for his Kanawha record.

Money Musk

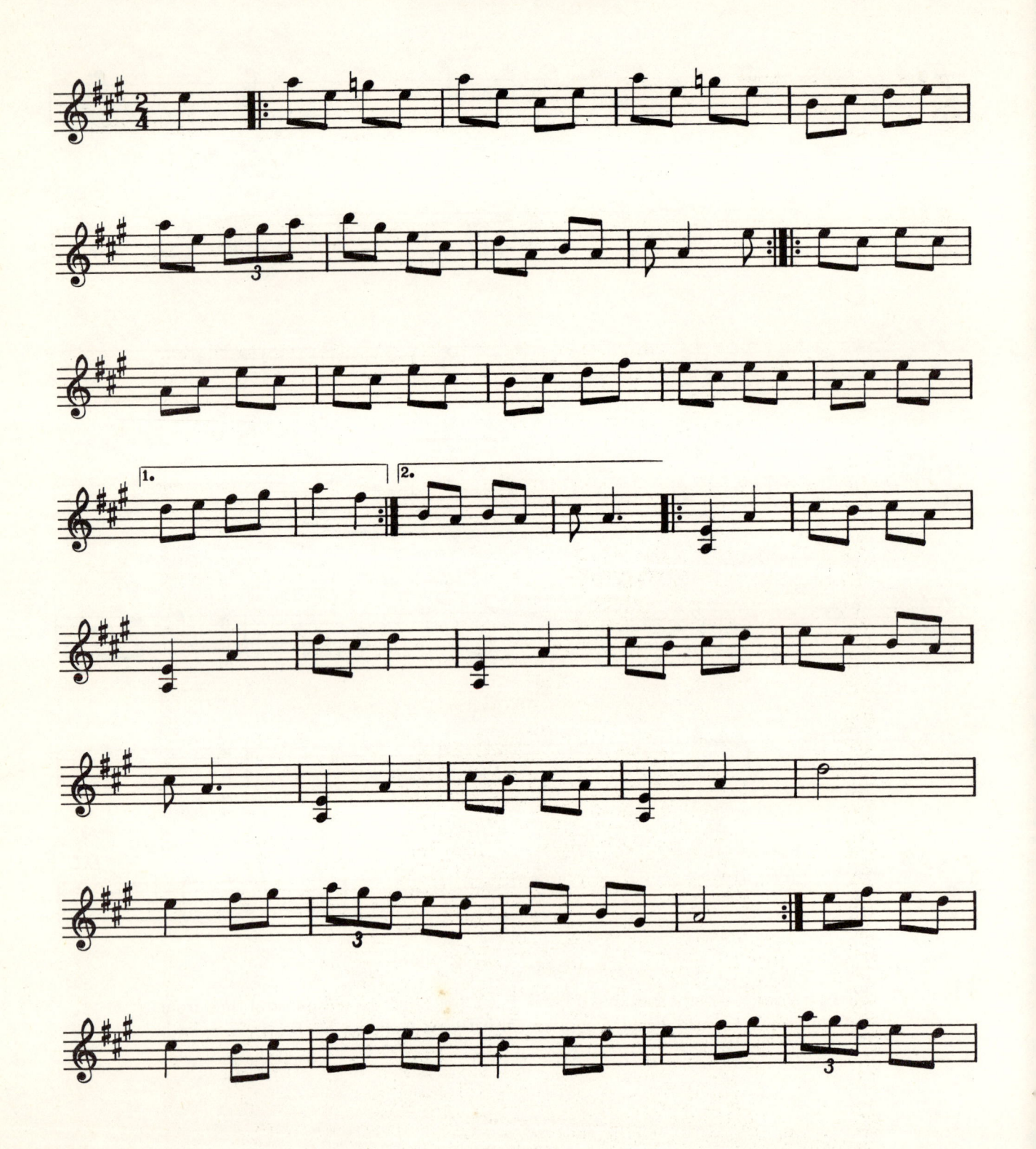

Money Musk is an old Scottish Reel that is still played in the British Isles and in New England. In the Southern Appalachians, the tune is very rare. The transcription here is based on how Henry Reed played the tune. It is a remarkable version, being wholly Appalachian in character and yet obviously descended from the Celtic originals.

Henry Reed

Fire on the Mountain

I first heard this tune played by Alan Block at the Union Grove Old Time Fiddlers' Convention in 1965. Kyle Creed and Fred Cockerham have recorded a nice version on County Records. Probably the version that has most influenced this transcription is the 78 recording made by Gid Tanner and the Skillet Lickers. Also, the low part has much in common with a 78 recording made by Pope's Arkansas Mountaineers called *Hog-eyed Man*.

Grey Eagle

This is one of the standard square dance tunes in the key of A. The transcription is based on Charlie Higgins' fine version.

There are not as many fiddle tunes played in the key of C as in the other major keys. However, at least two tunes in this key, *Billy In The Low Ground* and *Wagoner* are among the most common dance tunes played in the Appalachians. When playing in this key, be careful to finger F—second finger on the D string and first finger on the E string.

Billy in the Low Ground

This is one of my favorite tunes. I first learned it from a Burnett and Rutherford 78 record. Lowe Stokes, a North Georgia fiddler, has also recorded an interesting version which has been reissued by County Records. I have also heard an Irish version called *The Kerryman's Daughter*. Henry Reed played a tune called *Billy In The Lowground* in the key of G. The version that I like best was played by Charlie Higgins. Notice that there is an extra measure at the end of each part, making nine rather than the usual eight measure phrases. This is the way Uncle Charlie played the tune.

East Tennessee Blues

This is basically Charlie Higgins' version of a tune which is also called *Honeysuckle* or *Honeysuckle Rag*. Fred Price recorded a version for Folkways on the "Old Time Music at Clarence Ashley's" album. Also, the Camp Creek Boys, Kyle Creed's band, has recorded a version for County Records.

Wagoner

This transcription is based on Charlie Higgins' playing.

Row's Division

This rare tune sounds to me like an old march that may have been associated with a military group. I learned the tune from Dave Milefsky who had it from Alan Jabbour.

HORNPIPES

A hornpipe is a kind of Irish dance that is still being played in the British Isles. Hornpipes are written in $\frac{4}{4}$ time and played more slowly than a reel and with a much more exaggerated dotted or bouncy rhythm. In the Appalachians, hornpipes, strictly speaking, have lost their distinction. The Irish dance which fits the original way of playing the hornpipe rhythm is not done in the Appalachians. In general, most tunes that are called hornpipes are played in the same manner as reels and both are usually lumped together as breakdowns. However, since hornpipes were originally played at a slower tempo, many of the beautiful old tunes which fit this dance contained patterns of notes difficult to finger at faster tempos. The effect has been that in the Appalachians, hornpipes have become less common than reels. Many fiddlers can not play these tunes at the brisk tempos that have come to be associated with the Appalachian breakdown. Those fiddlers that do play them generally have to play at slightly slower tempos. Even so, hornpipes are usually played faster and less strictly than the Irish version.

It seems to be the case that fiddlers who like hornpipes tend to like them so much that often their style of playing breakdowns is influenced by their taste for hornpipes. Fiddlers of this sort tend to play all their tunes a little slower and more bouncy, and often relate the melody of their tunes to the kind of fingering found in the old strict hornpipe tunes. Another quality these fiddlers carry over to their playing of other tunes is a more independent bowing style than the more breakdown oriented fiddlers use. The result has been that in the Appalachians, a style of playing has developed concurrent with the mainstream breakdown style which may be termed the "hornpipe style" though it has little in common with the pure Irish hornpipe strictly played. Fiddlers who play this way are sometimes called "hornpipey fiddlers" although their repertory may include only a small number of tunes which are authentic hornpipes.

The tunes in this chapter are all hornpipes that are played in hornpipe style by Southern Appalachian fiddlers. All of them, with the exception of *George Booker*, are also played as strict hornpipes by Irish fiddlers.

Frank George

Fisher's Hornpipe

This is probably the most popular hornpipe played in the Southern Appalachians. Many fiddlers claim and some printed versions reflect that the tune was originally played in the key of F. I have rarely met a fiddler who played the tune in this key. Around Galax quite a few older fiddlers like Charlie Higgins, play *Fisher's* in the key of G. This version in the more common key of D, derives mainly from Frank George's manner of playing the tune.

Rickett's Hornpipe

Rickett's is also very popular in the Appalachians but slightly less so than *Fisher's* which is easier to play. The tune is also common in the British Isles. The Skillet Lickers recorded a version under the title of *Tanner's Hornpipe*. I originally learned the tune from Frank George.

Red Haired Boy

I first heard this tune played on a 78 by O'Leary's Irish Minstrels and loved it immediately. I played a version for Frank George and learned that the tune is well known in West Virginia as *The Old Soldier with a Wooden Leg*, or *Wooden Leg*. In Ireland this hornpipe is often called *Gildleroy* which is the Gaelic equivalent of *Red Haired Boy*. It is also known as *The Little Beggarman*. Irish fiddlers sometimes play a minor version of the tune noting C rather than C♯. Either way it's a beautiful tune.

Durang's Hornpipe

A very good version of *Durang's* can be heard on an old 78 record by Dan Massey and his family. This is one hornpipe that is even played by non-hornpipe style fiddlers. In these cases the crossbowing is usually not done. I learned most of this version from Frank George.

Sailor's Hornpipe

This version derives mainly from Frank George's playing.

George Booker

The high part of this tune is almost certainly a hornpipe. But the low part is not. Henry Reed played a version with a low part that is much more characteristic of hornpipes. I heard the tune first on Uncle Am Stuart's Vocalion 78 and later as played by Frank George. Somehow or other my playing of the low part sounded more minor and different from all three sources. But I have continued to play the tune this way because I like it as much as the other versions.

Mountain Hornpipe

I learned this tune from Alan Jabbour at the Galax, Virginia Old Fiddlers' Convention in 1965. Later, I heard a fine version played by Melvin Wine who took first prize in the Oldtimers' fiddle contest at the West Virginia State Folk Festival at Glenville in 1972.

Haste to the Wedding

This is not a hornpipe but a jig. Jigs are Irish dances in $\frac{6}{8}$ time and comparatively rare in the Southern Appalachians. *Haste To The Wedding* is one of the most popular jigs played all over the United States. When you play a jig, try to accent the first eighth note in each group of three. This is the way jigs can be lilted.

Discography

Highly Recommended

Kanawha
   307/ Traditional Music for Banjo, Fiddle, and Bagpipes. Franklin George and John Summers

Folk Promotions
   11567/ Old Time Songs and Tunes from Clay County, West Virginia. French Carpenter

AAFS
   L62/ American Fiddle Tunes, ed. by Alan Jabbour, Library of Congress Recording Lab

AAFS
   L2/ Library of Congress Recording Lab

Rounder
   0010/ The Fuzzy Mountain String Band

Rounder
   / Summer Oaks and Porch, The Fuzzy Mt. String Band

Rounder
   / Alan Jabbour, fiddle and Tommy Thompson, banjo

Also Recommended

County
   505/ Charlie Poole and the North Carolina Ramblers
   509/ Charlie Poole and the North Carolina Ramblers, vol. 2
   516/ The Legend of Charlie Poole
   506/ Gid Tanner and the Skillet Lickers
   507/ Old Time Fiddle Classics
   510/ Red Fox Chasers
   513/ Grayson and Whitter
   514/ Hell Broke Loose in Georgia
   517/ Texas Farewell
   518/ Echoes of the Ozarks, vol. 1
   519/ Echoes of the Ozarks, vol. 2
   520/ Echoes of the Ozarks, vol. 3
   524/ Da Costa Woltz's Southern Broadcasters
   701/ Clawhammer Banjo
   703/ Texas Hoedown
   705/ Virginia Breakdown
   707/ Texas Fiddle Favorites
   709/ Camp Creek Boys
   713/ Down at the Cider Mill. Jarrell, Cockerham, and Jenkins
   717/ More Clawhammer Banjo Tunes
   718/ Ernest East and the Pine Ridge Boys
   723/ Back Home in the Blue Ridge, vol. 2. Jenkins, Jarrell and Cockerham
   733/ The Legend of Clark Kessinger

Davis Unlimited
   DU 33002/ Train on the Island, Norman Edmonds

Folkways
   FA 2355/ Old Time Music at Clarence Ashley's, vol. 1
   FA 2359/ Old Time Music at Clarence Ashley's, vol. 2
   FA 2363/ Roscoe Holcomb and Wade Ward
   FA 2366/ Watson Family
   FA 2434/ 37th Old Times Fiddlers' Convention at Union Grove
   FA 2435/ Galax, Va. Old Time Fiddlers' Convention
   FA 2951/ Anthology of American Folk Music, vol. 1
   FA 2952/ Anthology of American Folk Music, vol. 2
   FA 2953/ Anthology of American Folk Music, vol. 3
   FS 3811/ Traditional Music from Grayson and Carroll Counties
   FS 3832/ Bluegrass from the Blue Ridge

Kanawha
   311/ The Hollow Rock String Band
   600/ The Kessinger Brothers

Biograph
   6003/ Original Bogtrotters, 1937-42

Columbia
   CS-9660/ Ballads and Breakdowns of the Golden Era

Victor
   LPV-552/ Early Rural String Bands

Historical
   8003/ Traditional Country Classics, 1927-1929
   8004/ Ernest V. Stoneman and his Dixie Mountaineers, 1927-28

Prestige/International
   INT 25003/ Ballads and Breakdowns from the Southern Mountains, Southern Journey 3

Tommy Jarrell